SKILFUL

SHOW
JUMPING

**Photography by
BOB LANGRISH**

Jane Holderness-Roddam

A & C Black · London

First published by
A & C Black (Publishers) Ltd
35 Bedford Row, London WC1R 4JH

© 1990 Jane Holderness-Roddam

ISBN 0 7136 3255 0

A CIP catalogue record for this
book is available from the British Library.

Typeset by Latimer Trend & Company Ltd, Plymouth
Printed and bound in Great Britain by
William Clowes Ltd, Beccles and London.

Acknowledgements
The author would like to thank
Pam Cary Croton for her prompt
typing of the manuscript and Bob
Langrish for his excellent photographs.

CONTENTS

INTRODUCTION

Show jumping is one of the most popular of all equestrian sports and can be enjoyed by young and old up to a certain standard on a variety of different types, sizes and breeds of horse.

Whether you just want to enjoy the competitive atmosphere at a fairly basic level or rise to the height of the international scene, be it on ponies or horses, there are classes for everyone, catering for every standard of horse and pony.

This book aims to encourage the horse and pony owner to take up the sport; it gives a thorough background to every aspect from caring for the horse and what is required to take up show jumping, through to the necessary training on the flat and over fences to be able to do this. Advice on jumping different types of fences and courses as well as on competing and how to plan your day are all included, along with general tips on problems that might occur and how to deal with them.

Throughout the book riders and horses are referred to in the third person singular as 'he'. This should of course be taken to mean 'he or she'.

History

Although the riding of horses has been going on for centuries, jumping as such was rarely a necessity whilst the British countryside was open, until the late eighteenth century. It was at this time that the Enclosure Act came in and people became aware of the necessity of being able to jump if they were still to cross the country. Once it was discovered how well the horse could jump, various 'leaping' contests were organised. These were mostly for or to settle disputes, but more and more started to take place at fairs around the country. Great stories of jumping feats in the hunting field spread and everyone realised that jumping added new dimensions to the enjoyment of riding.

It is unclear where the first official show jumping class took place, but that arranged in Paris in 1866 at a harness show seems to be the most likely. Other shows followed and by the end of the 1800s regular contests in Europe and the United States were established. Most of the classes were of a puissance type, with height being the only consideration, and some amazing performances were recorded of horses jumping over 2m ($6\frac{1}{2}$ft). Other contests started to appear, such as Derby-type courses, and a Dublin's farmer's course was introduced at Balls Bridge in 1881.

In the early days the 'backward seat' was used, which must have been quite uncomfortable for both horse and rider, especially when jumping such enormous fences. Thanks mainly to the Italian Frederico Caprilli, the 'forward seat' was introduced, and this became the adopted style as time went on. The horses at least must have been more than grateful that this style emerged early in the history of show jumping.

Show jumping became an Olympic sport in 1912 at Stockholm and has progressed enormously ever since; almost every equestrian nation in the world now holds competitions. There are now so many different types of class suitable for everyone that it is virtually impossible to mention them, except in general terms. It was at the time of the Olympic Games in Stockholm that the Federacion Equestre Internationale (FEI) was formed to set out rules standardising those already in use by participating nations. To this day the FEI governs all international show jumping and organises the calendar for all championships and competitions around the world.

In Britain the British Show Jumping Association (BSJA) is the governing body of national competitions. The British Equestrian Federation is responsible for co-ordinating all equestrian sport with the FEI; it attends their general assembly once a year to keep up to date with future policy and changes, and to ensure that Britain's riders are represented as and when necessary.

At the present time, HRH The Princess Royal is President of the FEI and it is fortunate that such a competent sportswoman is in a position to take an objective and positive role in steering the sport forwards, yet maintaining control on what is expected from the horses.

Competitions

Competitions of all types have been devised to test both horse and rider over courses that demand different qualities in various ways over a series of fences. The horses' jumping ability is tested and faults around the course are penalised, the winner being the one who incurs the least or no faults. In cases of equality there is normally a jump off to decide the winner, and in some classes this may involve two or even three jump offs over a shortened and/or heightened course. Otherwise the winner is decided on time.

Riders can choose classes to suit their horse's ability, and rules are laid down to ensure that only horses with certain qualifications may enter the bigger classes, thereby controlling the participation of the less experienced horses, until they have proved a certain degree of competence and experience.

The Pony Club is a marvellous place to learn the basics of all riding activities. Many top show jumpers started at Pony Club level

Types of competition

Every country has its own special national rules but all generally follow the same pattern and this book uses the British Show Jumping Association's rules as a general guide where appropriate. Show jumping competitions are judged and scored in a number of different ways and basically fall into three categories:

Competitions under Table A

In these, jumping faults are incurred as follows for errors made during a round: knock down, 4 faults; disobedience or refusal, 3 faults, or 6 for second time; fall, 8 faults; water jump, 4 faults. Time faults are incurred for each commenced second in excess of the time allowed.

Competitions judged under A5 have a course divided into two sections. The first section is judged under Table A, not against the clock but with a time allowed. A competitor who incurs any jumping or time faults over the first section must leave the arena immediately on completing the first section.

Competitors with a clear round over the first section remain in the arena until the judge rings the bell for the second, jump-off section of the course. This may include part of the first section but must have at least three other fences higher or wider than those in the first section.

Table C

For these, jumping and time faults are not incurred but four seconds is added for each knock down or for landing in the water or on the tape. First falls and first and second disobediences are not penalised. Time penalties are also incurred when an obstacle is displaced as the result of a refusal.

Special competitions

For these, the rules for scoring are as laid down for each competition and must be clearly printed in the schedules.

Top score

Riders jump fences worth a certain score within a set time. Fences may be jumped twice to score but do not score if they are knocked down.

Accumulator

Competitors jump a course consisting of six, eight or ten fences of progressive size and difficulty. Points are awarded for each fence cleared.

Table A			
	First round	First jump off	Second jump off
A1	Not against clock Equal winners qualify for first time jump off	Not against clock Equal winners qualify for second jump off	Not against clock Equal winners divide prize money
A2	Not against clock Equal winners qualify for first jump off	Not against clock Equal winners qualify for second jump off	Against clock Competitors placed on faults and time
A3	Not against clock Equal winners qualify for jump off	Against clock Competitors placed on faults and time	
A4	Against clock Competitors placed on faults and time		

The Puissance wall is easily cleared by Robert Smith and City Tycoon at The Royal International Horse Show

Jeff McVean clears the Puissance wall on Whisper Grey. Each horse has its own style of jumping this huge fence

Puissance

There are four to six large single fences and the competition is scored according to Table A. The jump offs can be extremely exciting as riders try for new records. There may be up to four jump offs, which take place over two single fences, one of which must be a wall. The jump offs are not against the clock.

Six bars

This comprises six identical, vertical bars on a straight line, with two non-jumping strides between each one. There may be up to four jump offs (not against the clock).

Knock out

This takes place as a knock-out tournament in which two competitors at a time compete simultaneously over separate courses. It is judged under Table C but with time penalties of two instead of four seconds.

Team

This is a competition for teams of three or four riders; only the best three scores count towards the total. It may be judged under Table A over two rounds (not against the clock), followed by one jump off against the clock, or under Table C. There is a drawn starting order.

Relay

This is a competition for two or more riders (as stated in the schedule) and is judged under Table C. The starting order must be drawn.

Rescue relay

This is for two competitors only, with points scored on a fault and out basis. As soon as a competitor makes one error, the bell is rung and his other team member (the rescuer) takes over at the next fence. Each team member continues to rescue the other until the course is completed. The competition is decided on points; if they are equal, it is decided on time from when the first competitor started until the last crossed the finishing line.

Qualifying competitions

There are numerous competitions that take place throughout the year that qualify the rider for further rounds and finals. The courses must be built strictly in accordance with the specifications laid down in the rules, and heights and spreads must not be exceeded. Such competitions cater for novices up to senior international standards as well as for juniors, young riders and adults. There are also indoor classes for the winter.

It is most important to thoroughly read the rules for each competition before entering so that you fully understand the competition and how it is to be judged. Each of these qualifying competitions has distinctive sponsors' rosettes and prize money as laid down for each class.

Racing for the finish: John Whitaker just beats Geoff Goodwin to the finish at Olympia

Indoor shows have tremendous atmosphere. This one at S'Hertogenbosch is no exception

To compete in competitions affiliated to the national body (BSJA in Britain), riders must be members of it and their horses must be registered. This applies generally to all countries and ensures uniformity of standards as well as keeps the sport up to date with results recorded on a national register. Through this, it is possible to keep records of winnings and prize money. It is possible when starting to find shows and classes that are not affiliated, and these can be useful to start with if they are well built and you want to get going a bit before becoming more serious about your chosen sport. Remember, however, that very often these shows and courses may be built by amateurs, and distances and turns, as well as fences themselves, can be far from ideal. Ask someone more experienced if the course looks suitable for you and your horse at this stage – you don't want to be put off before you get started! Once you are

confidently jumping courses with fences that are 84cm (2ft 9in) high, you might just as well become registered and work your way up through the ranks.

The right horse

We are assuming you have got your own horse or pony, but if you are thinking of taking up show jumping quite seriously, it is worth thinking now whether you have the right horse to take you as far as you wish to go, or whether he might be a bit limited for one reason or another and you should be thinking in terms of replacing him later on.

Ponies are amazing for their size. They can jump incredible heights if they are the jumping sort and many make wonderful schoolmasters for endless children who are growing up fast.

The Services Team Jumping Class at the Royal Windsor Horse Show is hotly contested every year and provides a most exciting competition

Everyone has to start somewhere and this junior rider is doing a great job in the mini-jumping at Olympia, being in a fair position over the parallel

Because some children grow much faster than others, it is difficult to decide when a bigger pony is required, but generally, if the pony appears to be ridden by someone who is too big, or in any way starts to go less well than he used to, it is likely that he is finding the weight or size of that child a bit much, and he should never be pushed to do more than he is physically able.

A horse needs to be well proportioned, with a strong 'back end' and hocks, as this is, after all, where the power must come from to jump those fences. He must have a good shoulder so that he can pick up well in front and be able to stretch forwards if necessary over a big fence. His back must be strong and well muscled; his legs must be hard; and his feet and joints must be designed to withstand the pounding that is inevitable for the show jumper. Above all, he

must have ability and enjoy jumping and be confident, courageous and careful enough to want to jump those all important clear rounds.

There are many horses who are good jumpers and who with careful training can go far. There are a few who are exceptional and who in the right hands can reach the very top. And there are an awful lot who are not very good, partly because they were never given the chance to develop their potential.

Every horse has the ability to jump height and spread, and for show jumping this is what is required. It is also necessary to improve the horse's technique so that he can make the very best of his natural ability to clear a course that demands agility as well as ability. How this is achieved is very much the responsibility of the rider. The horse can only be as good as the person who pilots him.

What you require

To do show jumping reasonably seriously you will need training facilities, the correct clothes and necessary equipment for horse and rider, and transport.

Training facilities

Training facilities should include a decent, flat area with good footing. Whether this is an arena, or a corner of a well-drained field, or someone else's indoor school, it doesn't matter – as long as you can use it two or three times a week to school the horse when he is up and fit. You will also need access to some decent jumps. Poles, to start with, help to improve agility, but once the horse is fit, and not before, you will need to be able to do some grid work and jump planks, walls, a gate, etc. as well as uprights and parallels made into a course. If you are short of fillers, then barrels, straw bales, etc. can be used to improvise as long as you are able to jump a decent course at some stage before going out to compete for the first time.

Horse and rider well turned out and happy in what they are doing

Most people will already have done this, so it will not be necessary as long as you have plenty of poles and uprights or standards with cups to work with when necessary.

There is little point in jumping when the ground is bad; it will do nothing for your horse and makes a mess of the ground. Look after your jumps by keeping them under cover if possible, or at least off the ground so that they do not rot. Poles left on wet ground will quickly deteriorate. Painting them regularly will help to protect them. Repair any damage immediately so that your fences last. Keep all cups together in a bucket or drum, preferably with a hole in the bottom so that they are less likely to rust. Never leave cups lying around for horses to injure themselves on.

Clothes

You will need a proper skull cap and harness that conform to the rules on dress and turnout.

Collars and ties or hunting stocks must be worn. Polo-neck sweaters are *not* allowed. With blue, black, red or green coats, only white stocks on white shirts and white ties are permitted. Coloured stocks are usual with tweed coats.

Spurs must not be longer than 3cm ($1\frac{1}{3}$in) and must only be worn with the shank pointing downwards. They must not be misused. Plastic spurs are forbidden. Whips must be between 45 and 75cm (18 and 30in) long and must not be weighted or have a hard point at the end.

Breeches and jodhpurs should be white, fawn or pale yellow. All clothes should be worn so that the rider looks neat and tidy in the arena.

Equipment

The horse will require suitable tack including a well-fitting saddle, bridle, breastplate and surcingle. He will need over-reach (bell) boots, some form of leg protection such as open-fronted brushing boots in front and

Preparing for the show involves putting everything ready and clean before loading into your horse box or trailer

The horse should be well protected for travelling with leg protectors or bandages, sufficient rugs for the temperature of the day and adequate tail protection

possibly some lighter ones behind, and studs for the different types of ground. It is always a good idea to have a few spare bits, nosebands and martingales in case the brakes are not working as well as you had hoped.

Transport facilities

Travelling gear to get you safely from A to B is essential, with enough rugs to cater for the extremes of hot and cold weather plus sweat rugs, waterproofs, coolers, etc. Travelling boots are quick and easy, but make sure they fit and stay in place. Any horse who is not a good traveller would be better with gamgee or other leg protection and bandages with knee caps, hock boots and poll guard to prevent him knocking himself if he moves about a lot.

The horse-box or trailer is essential and must be safe, strong and within legal requirements

on the road. Check your insurance, if you have a trailer, to ensure that this is covered by the small print. Make sure that your horse can travel comfortably. The pony trailer you started with may be quite unsuitable for your 16.2hh. horse.

Look into all these things carefully at the beginning of the season and make sure that you have registered your horse and renewed your membership before you intend to compete. If your horse is insured, check that he is covered for show jumping or that you don't want to increase cover to include anything more than you already have.

If you have all this under control, you can sit down, plan your season, decide what competitions you want to aim for, and set about working out how you intend to work up to include these in your programme.

GENERAL CARE OF THE HORSE

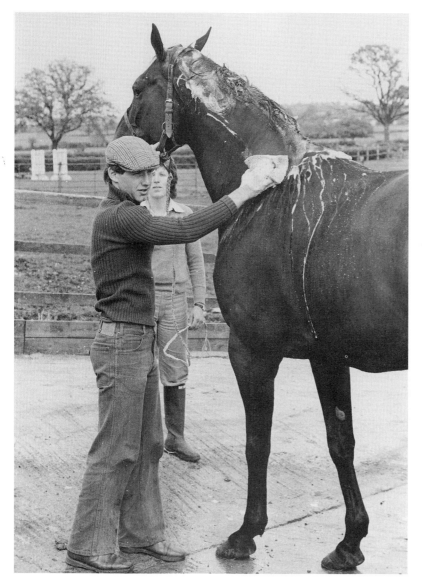

Horses should always be kept clean and tidy when stabled but a mane and tail wash will smarten them up before going to a show

The general care of and everyday attention to the horse plays a big part in future success in the ring. If he is not looked after, he will hardly be able to perform at his best. Very often it is not so much a case of what you do but how you do it that makes all the difference. You may go into one yard that seems to have all the facilities but where the horses look poor and unhappy, yet down the road at some relatively scruffy stables you will find that the horses are doing well, looking good and jumping well.

There are several reasons for this situation, and more often than not it is the attention to important details that matters rather than a lot of endless fussing. The horse, like a human, needs exercise, food and rest and as long as he has enough of these three basics he should be essentially fairly happy with his lot. There are, however, a few other important aspects of general care that need attention at regular intervals and these include worming, teeth care, shoeing and certain vaccinations to be seen to

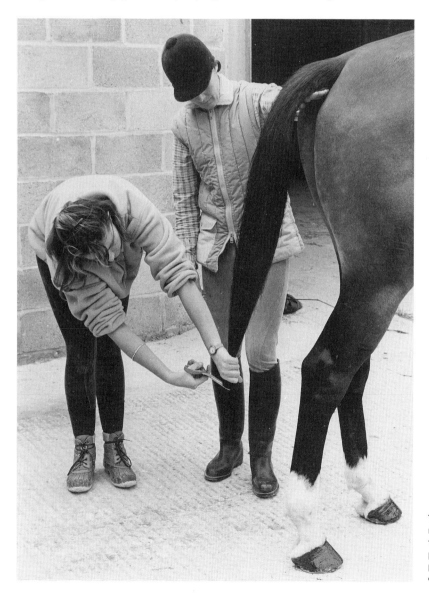

Trimming and tidying of manes and tails ensures that your horse looks the part. There are often prizes for the best turned out horse and rider

All horses enjoy some relaxation in the field. If it is cold or wet a New Zealand rug will be the answer. Make sure the leg straps are secure and fitted correctly

at suitable times of the year. All this must be fitted in around the horse's programme.

Feeding

The importance of a daily routine cannot be overstressed but this can easily be worked out to fit into your own particular life-style. Try to stick to regular feed times and to feed your horse according to the work he is doing.

It is vital to treat each horse as an individual and to work out from his appearance whether he will need more. An overfat horse is going to find it more difficult to jump big fences than one who is looking well and fit. On the other hand, one in poor condition does no one any credit, will tire easily and should not be asked to do too much until his condition has improved.

The principles of feeding should be followed at all times. The following covers the most important points:

1 feed little and often. The horse has a tiny stomach in relation to his size and cannot accommodate big feeds well

2 feed according to the work being done. Study your horse to get an idea of what suits him and how much he needs to keep the right sort of condition

3 always cut down on food, particularly all concentrates, if the horse is not being worked, has a day off or is ill

4 avoid making any sudden changes to the diet or routine

5 do not work a horse fast just after he has been fed. This will affect his breathing and could also cause colic

6 make sure fresh, clean water is always available, but do not allow the horse to have a long drink before strenuous work.

Feeding is a great art and not just a matter of putting in a scoop of this or that. Each horse should be treated as an individual and his likes and dislikes taken into account

Types of food

Oats

There are several types of food on the market for the horse but oats are traditionally considered to be the best all-round food available. They are best fed lightly bruised, being easier to digest, and are usually fed with a little bran and a good handful of chaff.

Barley

Barley is a useful substitute for oats as it is less heating than oats and so is less likely to 'hot up' the horse. Boiled barley is excellent for tired horses and is a good fattening food. It must be boiled and simmered for four to six hours until the grains split.

Bran

Bran is useful for bran mashes, which are generally fed quite warm and wet. Bran mashes should be given once or twice a week before rest days or whenever the horse is off work or just to clear his system a little. To make a bran mash, pour boiling or very hot water over your bran so that it is fairly wet. Add Epsom salts or salt and a handful of oats or mix for interest (boiled food is a good inclusion) and allow to stand until it has cooled sufficiently to be fed. Bran mash has a good laxative effect and is excellent for the invalid horse. It can, however, be harmful if fed in large quantities, affecting both growth and health.

Chaff

Chaff is usually a mixture of hay and straw given to add bulk to feeds and is often now mixed with a small amount of molasses.

Cubes or nuts

Cubes or nuts are compound mixtures of a variety of different ingredients and are made up of different formulae, based mainly on the protein content. These vary from the Racehorse Cube to the Horse and Pony Cube and Grass Nut. Cubes have certain advantages in that they are specially formulated with the necessary vitamins etc., and the well-known proprietary brands are reliable. Cubes should be fed with bran and chaff and often take the place of oats in the diet, especially if the horse tends to hot up.

Sugar beet

Sugar beet pulp or nuts are an excellent source of energy and roughage and are good for putting on weight. Sugar beet *must* be well soaked for at least eight to twelve hours, as it expands to up to six times its dry volume. It is essential that it is fully soaked before being fed, as if it continues to swell up in the stomach the results could be horrific. Once soaked, sugar beet should be fed within 24 hours, so do not soak more than you need.

Coarse mix

Coarse mixes are becoming increasingly popular and, like cubes, are made up into different levels of protein formulations. They contain a variety of foods such as oats, barley, molasses, beans, peas, etc. as well as additives. Be sure to obtain the right formulation for the type of work your horse is doing. These mixes are generally fed as a single feed with no other one added.

Salt

Salt is an essential part of the horse's diet and should be added to the feed daily if salt licks are not already supplied. Extra salt should be given in hot weather.

Apples and carrots

Don't forget that your horse will appreciate apples and carrots, or the cuttings and scrapings from them, as a change whenever these are available. Always cut these up, making sure that this is done lengthwise so that they do not get stuck in the horse's throat.

Hay

Good-quality hay makes up most of the roughage content in the diet and this should always be of good quality, sweet smelling and not musty. Hay will anyway only be as good as the land from which it has come but if this is up to standard and the hay has been well made, it will provide a good base to the diet and take the place of grass. Generally hay should be freely available but this will depend on the horse. The greedy ones will need to be restricted, and if the horse is getting overfat, hay should be reduced.

If your horse tends to cough, soaking the hay overnight and then hanging it up to drain for 10 minutes before feeding will usually overcome this problem. Horsehage or vacuum-packed hay may also reduce the problem, which is usually associated with dust.

So much of the art of feeding depends on how you do it, and it is important to mix all feeds well and damp them as necessary. A mixture of warm water and molasses used on the feeds three or four times a week is generally appreciated and adds variety.

Worming

It will make little difference how much food you give your horse if he is not being kept regularly

Worming is a very important aspect of horse care and should be carried out approximately every six weeks throughout the year. It can be given in paste form as seen or in the feed

wormed. The worms will flourish but the horse will not! Every horse should be wormed at intervals of six to eight weeks and if there are other horses or the paddocks are always full of horses, this should be done every four weeks.

Worming is best done after discussing with your vet the brands and doses of treatment that are available. There are certain times of the year when some worms such as bots are more common (depending on the country and climate). An extra dose at such times will help to ensure that your horse's worm burden (which is always present to some degree) does not get out of hand. Always worm all horses together who are likely to be going out in the same paddock, to help to prevent re-infestation. Paddocks should be rested for at least six months if possible to enable the land to clear itself of worms.

Teeth

These should be checked by your vet or horse dentist at least every year, some people preferring to do it every six months. They need rasping not just so that the horse can masticate his food better, but also to ensure that there are no hooks cutting into the cheeks, making the horse sore in the mouth and the discomfort affecting his way of going.

Many vets are notoriously bad at realising this second point, especially if they do not ride themselves.

Shoeing

This is particularly important, especially for the competition horse who is going to land from some height onto his front legs and take off from his hind ones over big fences. The horse must be safe and not slip and his feet should be kept in the correct shape so that the minimum of strain is put on his tendons. Allowing the toes to become too long is one of the main faults. Shoe regularly every three to four weeks either with removes or a new set as necessary. Study your horse's movement and discuss with

your farrier how to minimise problems and help to prevent unnecessary knocks. Setting in a shoe slightly or feather edging it can prevent silly knocks and brushing, whilst rounding the toes can be helpful in preventing over-reaching and excessive wear at this point.

As it is vital that your horse does not slip on turns into his fences etc., it is most important that he is given every help possible, so regular shoeing and the wearing of studs whenever jumping on anything other than really good ground makes sense. Large studs on wet or slippery ground and small ones on the hard are considered to be the best. There are numerous ones on the market.

Keep stud holes clean by filling them up with well-oiled cotton wool as soon as the horse has been shod. This can be picked out with a nail and any debris can be cleared with a sharp 'blow out'. Remove studs after use and refill with new oiled cotton wool.

Leg care

Care of the legs is essential to success and the legs should be checked daily to ensure that the slightest problem is detected early and can be acted on before it worsens.

Boot rubs

Boot rubs are one of the most common problems. Look at what is causing this: it may be that the boot is too small or large for the leg; that it has become stiff and needs a thorough oiling and cleaning; or is old and no longer doing the job it was designed for and instead is accentuating the problem. Sort this out and prevent if from becoming worse. Treat cuts, knocks and bruises straight away by washing the leg if necessary and cleaning out cuts or nicks with a mild antiseptic. Wound powder or an antiseptic spray should deal with most minor injuries.

Shoes

Watch out that clenches (nail ends) are not coming up on the shoes and causing a knock or

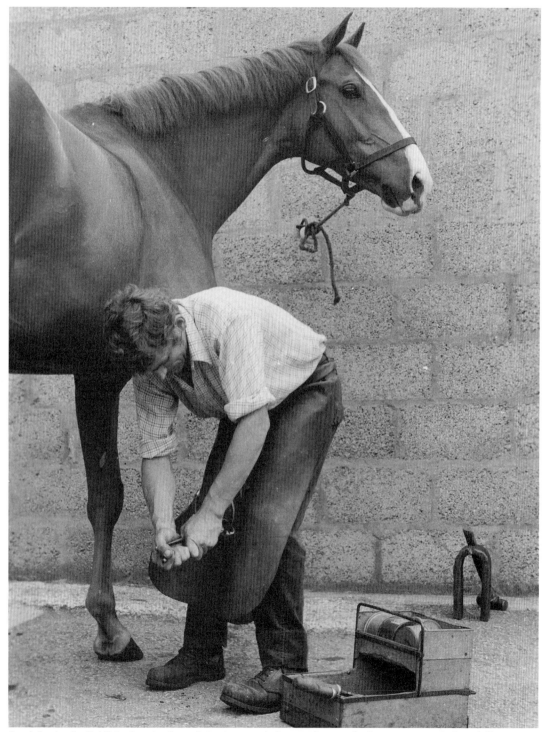

Good shoeing is vital if the jumping horse is to stay sound. Arrange for your farrier to come regularly and discuss whether stud holes are to be used or any corrective shoeing is necessary

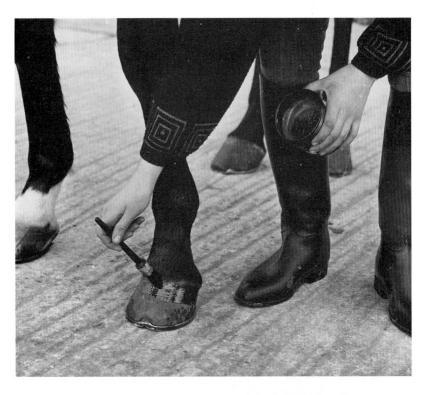

The foot takes a lot of strain in the jumping horse and must be well cared for with regular shoeing and good hoof care. Oiling will prevent brittleness and keep the coronet band supple

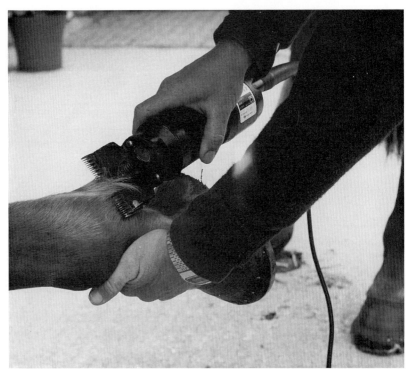

Using the clippers to trim heels and jaw will keep your horse looking tidy. A sharp pair of scissors will also do a very good job

bruise on the other leg and that the shoe is not spreading. Look at how the shoes are being worn – it can indicate a problem somewhere else if one shoe is becoming more worn than the other.

Inflammation

Heat in the leg can be a sign of inflammation and needs thorough investigation, especially when both legs are not a pair. If the horse flinches to pressure or if one leg is swollen, especially in the vicinity of the tendons, call your vet at once to find out whether or not this is serious and then treat accordingly. Any inflammation or pain associated with bruising is best treated immediately with ice or cold water to help to constrict blood vessels and minimise bruising. Inflammation due to pus or abscess formation requires hot poulticing to draw out the inflammation.

The heels

Cracked heels can make the horse very sore and these are generally caused by soreness in the heel area due either to lack of care, such as not cleaning or drying this area sufficiently if it gets wet or muddy continually, or to 'heel bug'. This condition is believed to be caused by either a virus or an allergy to certain types of ground.

In either case, it is important to clean the area thoroughly and to remove any scabby tops. This can be done with pure soap and warm water, rinsing thoroughly and drying with a clean towel before applying a good antiseptic or healing cream. Keep off the wet ground as much as possible. Bandaging with an animalintex poultice can be good in acute stages. Keep the heels well trimmed so that they dry quickly and easily.

The hocks

The hocks in the jumping horse can be prone to strain. These are the joints that are taking the initial strain as the horse thrusts himself upwards over the jumps, and they also have to cope with the quick turns etc. that are imposed on them during a jumping round. Watch out for any heat or swelling in this area that could denote strain. Thoroughpins and curbs can develop if too much strain is put on the hocks, especially in the young horse or before full fitness is achieved.

Windgalls

Windgalls are fairly common in jumpers and appear as soft swellings along the fetlock joints. Generally caused by jarring, they are not usually too serious in themselves but should be taken as a warning that the legs are feeling a bit of strain. They particularly tend to come up in hot weather when the going becomes hard, and are more obvious at the end of the season than at the beginning. Stable bandages give support and the legs should be watched and treated systematically; avoid overjumping if the ground is hard.

Splints

Splints often appear on young horses who are doing too much work on hard ground. Again these are warnings that young legs take time to harden, and horses should not be overworked too soon. Be guided by your vet's advice and ease off work whilst these are forming. Generally as long as they do not develop up high and interfere with the knee joint and ligaments round this, they cause little trouble once they have formed and hardened. You may well have to ease off work completely if lameness or inflammation is present.

Fitness

The importance of getting the horse properly fit and muscled up so that he can cope with the demands of the sport cannot be over-emphasised. Show jumping is demanding, albeit for short periods, and if the horse is not to be overstrained during this time of concentrated effort, it is vital that he is properly prepared to cope with the courses with the minimum of strain.

The early fitness starts, as it does for any horse, with walking, preferably on the hard, even surface of a road or good track. This should continue for two to three weeks,

Hacking out is important for all horses to give them a break from schooling or, if necessary, to improve their fitness

building up from half an hour a day to one and a half or two hours at the end of the second week. Make the horse walk out well so that he is exercising every muscle, and after the first week or two introduce a few hills into your rides if possible. Avoid very steep ones until the horse is really fit, but gradual ones are excellent for improving fitness and muscle tone.

Gradually introduce trotting and keep this as slow as possible so that the horse's muscles really have the chance to contract and relax with each stride. It is this that really builds up muscle power. Ideally, the horse should have at least six weeks, and preferably longer, of slow work before being expected to jump a fence.

It may not be possible to use the roads for the build up to fitness for one reason or another. This could be because it is simply not safe to do so in your area, the horse is bad in traffic, or there are no suitable roads to ride on in the area. In this case, stick to walk and slow trotting on large circles to start with in an arena or on some good ground where the horse will not slip around too much. It is best to do short periods of trotting and then relax in walk before going off and doing more work again. Don't overtire unfit muscles, but do a bit more week by week, asking the horse to use himself with greater collection as time goes on.

After the fourth or fifth week, introduce trotting poles, or cavaletti, to increase suppleness. Exercises on these will be included in the next chapter. They help to improve muscle tone and general fitness.

Cantering needs to be started around the fifth or sixth week, when the horse can be schooled on the flat more seriously between hacks out on the road. Try to do half an hour on the roads or slowly to get the circulation

going before doing any strenuous exercises on the flat or over poles. Canter large circles to start with and then build up on the various exercises to increase suppleness and obedience, remembering that this is the most important pace for the show jumper. All his work is done at this pace, but that does not mean that the walk and trot should be ignored, as he must be able to use all muscles correctly in preparation for every eventuality.

General routine

The stable routine is obviously extremely important and every detail must be remembered, as it is the little things that make the big difference between success and failure.

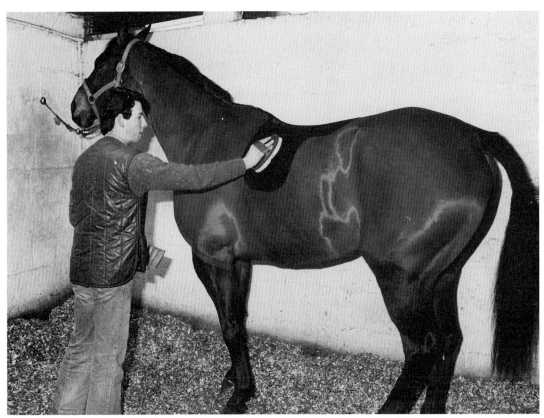

Grooming stimulates the skin and improves the coat. Clipping is essential if the coat is thick or long and makes it easier to keep the stabled horse in good condition

Very often it is not what is done but how it is done that is so important. Feeding has already been discussed. Grooming will keep the coat looking good and add a little stimulation to the skin as well as allow you to study your horse daily to ensure there are no indications of sore backs, rubs or skin problems.

Warmth and ventilation

Rugs should be well fitting and the horse should have enough on to keep him warm in cold weather. A cold horse uses up his stores of energy to keep warm and so will not 'do' as well as a warm one. Check his ears: if these are cold then your horse is cold. It is no good feeling his skin generally as the horse's temperature at 37.5°C (100.5–101°F) is relatively hotter than a human's anyway. An overheated horse is going to dehydrate and get a dry skin and may show up with heat lumps, so take off a rug and cut down the food a bit.

Make sure the horse is never left in a draught. This can affect the long back muscles and really make the horse quite stiff. It is best to always have a rug or sheet over the back in the

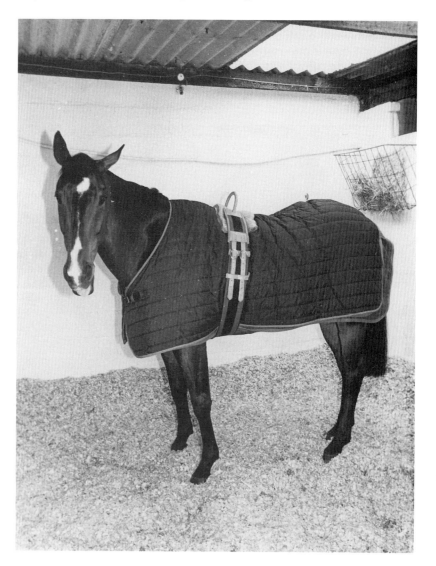

Your horse deserves good care with a warm, clean bed (this one is on shavings) and with good quality hay and food

stable when the horse is in work, except in very hot climates.

Make sure there is adequate ventilation in your stables, which should be light and airy. Windows should be open if possible, as long as these are safe, and any air vents should be kept free from dust and cobwebs so that they are effective. Cobwebs can really reduce the flow of air, so keep these to a minimum. Keep windows clean to let in as much light as possible, as the stabled horse misses out on light compared to those at grass.

It is rather misguided to shut the horse in at night and reduce the airflow unless the weather is really diabolical or the air blows into the stable badly. It is much better to add an extra rug and let the horse see what is going on than to coop him up in something reminiscent of a cell.

Boredom for the stabled horse can lead to problems such as weaving, cribbing and windsucking. If possible, try to turn the horse out for part of the day to relax and stretch his legs, as well as to give him the opportunity of eating some grass. If you can't do this, lead him out whenever possible and break up the day a bit with the various chores spread a little throughout the day.

Weaving

A weaving horse is one that persists in swinging his head, neck and forehand from side to side and/or rocking from foot to foot. Weaving can be reduced by use of an anti-weaving grill on the door, but this is not totally satisfactory, and the weaving horse in view of others can quickly lead to the vice being copied. Keep the weaver out of the sight of other horses or shut him in at times when this happens, such as feed times, when he should, of course, be fed first. Weaving, whilst annoying and the sign of a horse under stress or generally uptight, is the least serious of the vices.

Crib biting and windsucking

Crib biting is another easily caught vice whereby the horse grabs hold of something such as the top of the door or manger. It inevitably leads to the more dangerous vice of windsucking, whereby the horse gulps in air as he grabs the door or other object. This, of course, does the horse no good at all and can lead to colic and loss of condition in severe cases.

A cribbing strap can help to prevent this problem. This is designed in such a way that the horse cannot swallow without discomfort except with his head down, so he can eat as long as the feed is on the floor or low down, but cannot gulp with his head up. Cribox, a foul-tasting ointment smeared over such areas that are likely to be cribbed at, may discourage mild cases. Removing articles that can be grabbed and fitting a grill to the door will stop the habit at home. Once established, this habit is very difficult to stop and even when you turn the horse out, he will often continue to crib on the fence.

Flu and tetanus vaccinations

Protection against flu and tetanus is up to the owner but any responsible person can understand the importance of both of these. Most shows of any standing now make vaccination certificates a compulsory requirement for entries and no recognised racehorse stables will allow a horse near the premises without flu cover. Tetanus can rear its head at any time, following an often insignificant cut or wound, and cover can be given at the same time as your flu injections.

To be effective and acceptable, flu injections need to be given strictly in accordance with the recognised rules laid down by the Jockey Club and other societies. At present, these state that: 'The horse must receive two injections for primary vaccinations against Equine Influenza given no less than 21 days apart and not more than 92 days apart. In addition, a booster injection must be recorded as having been given no less than 150 and no more than 215 days after the second injection of the primary injection. An annual booster injection must then be given at intervals of not more than one year apart thereafter. These details must be recorded on the horse's identity chart which must undeniably relate to that horse to be signed and stamped by the vet if it is to be an acceptable document recognised everywhere.'

General cleanliness

General cleanliness around the yard is just as necessary as care of the horse, as the one will affect the other. All buckets should be regularly washed out once or twice a week; all feed bins should be rinsed out well after each feed. Fixed mangers should be scrubbed out periodically with disinfectant, salt, or soda crystals and water and then rinsed off thoroughly and wiped out as necessary. Any stale feed should be thrown out. Always thoroughly disinfect mangers, tops of doors, buckets etc. when you have a swap over of horses, to ensure that no germs or minor infections are passed on to the successor.

If there have been any infections or contagious problems in any of the stables, thoroughly disinfect the whole box, work tools, wheelbarrows, feedbins, buckets, haynets, grooming kit, etc., not forgetting rugs, rollers and headcollars, tack, numnahs, girths, etc. If possible, isolate any animal who is sick and avoid doing more to him than necessary. Remember to wash your hands and that your clothes might well be infected too. Keep set buckets, feedbins, grooming kit, tack, etc. for each horse and avoid unnecessary contact altogether.

Keep drains flowing free and, if they are smelly, add disinfectant and try to cure the cause. Keep them clear of debris so that they can do the job intended for them. Keep your muckheap neat and tidy; it will take up less room if you keep it orderly. Check that your wheelbarrow tyres are working and that they are kept oiled and effective.

Muck out your stables properly, shifting the bedding throughout the box daily regardless of the type of bedding used so that it stays fresh and there is no likelihood of dampness rotting wooden partitions.

Safety

This cannot be overemphasised.

Electricity

Electrical appliances and wiring must be treated as a safety priority and no switches, wires or sockets should be exposed and capable of being touched or chewed by the horse. Electrical shocks and fires have caused numerous deaths of horses, so it is your own responsibility to ensure that all is safe and secure.

Mangers of whatever type must be kept clean. A fussy feeder will quickly go right off his food if there is stale food left around

Mucking out is part of the daily care of the horse. A skip should be kept handy to pick up droppings throughout the day

Fire-fighting equipment

Fire-fighting equipment should be in every stable and easily accessible. Make sure you discuss details with any staff or users of the premises so that there is a plan known to everyone. Hoses and buckets should be easily located and a simple fire drill should be displayed prominently. Smoking should be forbidden in the stable area.

Sharp objects

The horse is a past master at finding something to injure himself on and it is necessary to have eyes everywhere and to be able to spot potential hazards before they arise. Protruding nails, holes in the floor, wire in the fences, broken glass – they can all lead to a problem for the accident-prone horse.

Feeding

Make sure anyone who is likely to use the feed room understands the importance of soaking sugar-beet pellets and knows which these are and what they look like. If there is likely to be any doubt, clearly mark the bag or bin they are in. Make sure that everyone realises the importance of cutting down on food when a horse is off work, otherwise you will have colic and azoturia on your hands.

Safety in the arena

Make sure your arena is safe, and if jumping make sure that the entrance is closed. Only jump if someone else is around, just in case of accidents. Never take risks with distances, strides etc. with a young horse. Don't jump fences with false ground lines. Remove cups from the jumps if they are jutting out and could catch a horse. Make sure you have sufficient control for what you are intending to do.

Be careful in windy weather that rugs etc. don't blow up and around the horse's head, causing him to panic. A horse really panicking becomes totally insensitive and will charge blindly anywhere and everywhere.

Above all, be on the lookout and remember that prevention is better than cure and the better you prepare your horse, the more chance there is of succeeding in the end.

FLAT WORK AND BASIC TRAINING

However brilliant your horse or pony, there will come a time when he could do a lot better with specialised training, and the sooner this can be started the quicker the results will show. If you are bringing on a youngster, this will all have started from the day you first rode him, but for one who has come to you later on, there may well be a lot to be done. To get the very best out of that animal may require weeks of patient retraining and time so that you and the horse start to build up real trust in each other to create that all-important partnership.

The most essential element to do this is absolute obedience. The horse must respond immediately and this will only be achieved if he is obedient to the rider's wishes. The horse must listen and respond and the rider must strive for greater success through sheer hard work. Unfortunately, there are no real short cuts on the road to the top.

Road work is important for hardening tendons when the horse first starts in work

Every horse must be supple and athletic enough to perform over the fences willingly and with ease. At the lower levels, this is quite straightforward, but as you progress, the horse needs to be trained to cope with the extra height and the more demanding courses and to develop a certain handiness that is essential to keep him going around the courses.

Flat work

Flat work must include work on all three paces, with particular emphasis placed on the following: the ability to shorten and lengthen the stride; turns, so that the approaches to the fences become easier; and exercises that will strengthen the horse and help him generally to jump better.

Basic paces

Walk and trot

Work on acquiring the good rhythm firstly at walk and trot. This cannot be achieved unless the horse is in balance, has been pushed up off his forehand and can carry himself, so that you can then concentrate on establishing an even and definite rhythm. Insist quietly on getting the horse into an outline and building on whatever natural paces are already there. Keep the leg on all the time, remembering to work on your own position at the same time. Get the weight down into the heel so that you have a firm position and deep seat. The position of the rider is vital when it comes to jumping the bigger fences. Sit up and ride forwards with confidence.

Once you can perform a good, balanced trot, practise your transitions from one pace to another so that the horse is able to change pace and re-establish balance in either as soon as possible. Remember to ease the hand forwards slightly to allow the horse that necessary freedom to take the first important step so that he can move on in a certain pace without having to throw up his head to get enough rein to do so. It is an elementary but nevertheless very important point to release and allow the

horse to go forwards. So often you see riders restricting their horses to such a degree that the horse simply cannot move forwards, yet they are still kicking at them. The horse really has only two alternatives – backwards or upwards – so be sympathetic with your hands and always think what it is that you are asking your horse to do. Does it make sense to him, and is it possible, in fact, to do it at all? Some people are that insensitive to an animal's make and shape that they fail to realise that certain things are not, in fact, logical!

Canter

In canter you are going to have to create more and more balance as time goes on. The young horse will take time to fully mature and will probably be slightly on his forehand anyway. Work at transitions from one pace to another and get the horse going up and down from trot to canter with ease. If he leans on the bit, this usually indicates that you have not used enough leg and have perhaps not really got the horse up together enough anyway.

You may need to come back to walk, use a stronger leg and push the horse more up together before continuing. The canter must be in a correct three-time sequence so that a correct rhythm is maintained. The horse must be going truly forwards onto the bit in rhythm and should be working at lengthening and shortening the stride a little as well as doing circles from 20m (66ft) to 10m (33ft) on his way around the track. Keep the horse together a bit more and use extra leg to contain him between hand and leg as greater demands are placed upon him. Make sure that you are still able to drop back a pace to get a good rhythm established with ease as well as to go up. Sometimes one thing will improve and another deteriorate unless you keep working at it. Let the horse walk between work periods to enable him to stretch his muscles well. This is important during all schooling. However fit, every horse needs to stretch and relax periodically.

Once you have managed to get your horse responding well to lengthening and shortening, it is time to build up obedience so that you can do tight turns such as will be required in the

This is a nice relaxed canter for a young horse but the rider will need to push the horse together a lot more so that the horse is balanced more on his hocks before jumping a big fence

arena. One way of doing this is to canter down the middle of the arena and turn into the outside track until your turn at the bottom is about 5 or 6m (16½ or 20ft). The horse will need to be quite collected to be able to achieve this, so prepare him by shortening the stride with a couple of half halts before you attempt the turn.

Pirouettes

Pirouettes are useful exercises to increase balance, rhythm and impulsion. The pirouette is a half or full circle on two tracks whereby the forehand moves around the quarters. It can be performed in walk or canter. To do this in walk, the horse must be slightly bent in the direction in which he is to go and must maintain good impulsion and remain on the bit throughout. Start with a small circle and gradually decrease

the size until the horse can perform the movement correctly so that the circle is no longer than the length of the horse.

Shoulder-in

In shoulder-in, the horse is bent around the rider's inside leg, looking *away* from the direction in which he is travelling. The horse, who should be at an angle of approximately 30 degrees, should move on three tracks. The horse's inside foreleg comes in onto the inside track; the inside hind leg and outside front leg move on the middle track with the outside hind on the outside track.

This is probably the most useful movement in all training of horses as it is asking all parts of the body to work in balance and collection. It increases the movement of the inside hind leg, requiring the horse to flex all his joints well on this side whilst the outside of the body has to stretch a little and become more supple to maintain the curve.

As with all exercises, only ask for a little bend to start with until the horse understands what is required. Perform the movement in walk to start with along the long side of the arena, just after you have turned a corner. In this way you should start with the correct bend. As soon as you have got the feel of the movement with your horse in walk, then work at it in trot, asking for just a few steps to start with and then riding the horse strongly forwards. It is most important that forward impulsion is maintained throughout. Keep thinking 'Forwards then bend, forwards then bend'. If the horse brings his head around too far, control this with greater contact on the outside rein and keep your inside leg forward to maintain bend and the outside leg further back, stopping the quarters from swinging out.

Travers and renvers

Travers and renvers again ask for the horse to be bent around the inside leg, but for these the horse looks *towards* the direction in which he is going. Again, start in walk and do the exercises down the long side or up the centre line of the arena. Start travers (quarters-in) out of the corner but keep the bend to the inside and, using the outside leg well behind the girth, ask the horse to bend sideways while maintaining forward movement with the inside leg only, strong enough to stop the quarters coming in too much. Remember to start all movements with a half halt to balance the horse.

For renvers, the situation is reversed and the quarters stay on the outside track whilst the rider brings the horse's shoulder in from the track. The outside leg is then used on the girth to bend the horse, and the inside leg behind the girth to keep the quarters on the track. The outside rein asks for flexion towards the way the horse is going and the inside rein controls the shoulders and maintains balance.

Halt and rein back

The halt and rein back are important movements that are necessary for the show

jumper to master. The halt is one of the most important lessons for the horse to learn. He must learn to stand and then to move forwards again. A young horse is unlikely to stand square until he has really mastered self-carriage and balance. He will gradually improve as his hind legs get more underneath him so that his weight is generally more squarely distributed.

Start the rein back by preparing the horse to readjust his balance, and think of what is being expected of him. It should not be attempted until the horse is reasonably obedient and supple. First of all, come to a balanced halt with the horse on the bit. Apply the legs for the horse to move forwards but restrict him to stop forward movement. As he steps back, ease the hands slightly, and then ask again, keeping the legs on lightly. Walk the horse forwards as soon as he has responded. If the horse fails to respond, it can be helpful to walk him into a railed, or better still boarded, corner. As he cannot go forwards, he is more likely to step back. Be quick to reward and praise when progress is made and keep the hands supple and soft, never hard so the horse resists. A helper on the ground can help by pushing with straight fingers into the horse's chest as each stride is asked for. It may take some horses a day or two to understand what is expected of them, but work first on achieving a soft and supple halt. Relax before asking for the step back, then when he responds, reward him by walking forwards.

Pole work

Pole work helps to make the horse supple and increase his balance and can be very useful in developing co-ordination and power in the show jumper. There are numerous exercises that can be performed over poles at the walk, trot and in canter. To begin with, it is best to start with the poles in a straight line set at suitable distances for your horse's stride. Generally, trotting poles are placed at a distance of around 1.2–1.4m (4ft–4ft 6in) from each other.

Poles generally encourage the horse to lower his head, which in turn allows the back to be used with greater effect and suppleness. Keep the horse calm and relaxed, varying the routine so that you turn and twist through as well as

The halt is one of the first things a horse must learn and is used throughout his training. Obedience is essential if horse and rider are to progress well together

Poles on the ground encourage suppleness and, for the young horse, are an excellent introduction to jumping

Raised poles make the horse work hard, as can be seen by comparing this photograph with the previous picture

over the poles to keep the horse's attention. If the horse tends to rush at the poles, circle him away and then gradually ask him to trot over one or two, then circle away again. Make him listen to what you are asking and keep changing direction so that he stops thinking about rushing and starts to concentrate on what he is doing.

Work on turning into and over the poles. You can do circles over two or three on one rein and then change to do a similar amount on the other rein. You can turn to the right over one lot and then left over another – there are all sorts of varieties you can work out and do, remembering not to be too abrupt as you change from one rein to another.

Cavaletti, or raised poles, will improve the action of the horse, making him use himself more as he steps higher over them. Poles put on blocks that have been scooped out to prevent them rolling around are good. The old type of cavaletti, with crossed ends, is now considered unsafe as the poles can roll if hit by the horse and could cause an accident.

Lungeing

Lungeing is a useful way of working the horse without a weight on his back. It can be done at any time during the horse's training and for a variety of reasons: in the early schooling of the horse, as a means of exercise; to retrain a spoiled horse; to allow the horse to 'let off steam' before more serious work; and lastly, as a means of training and improving the rider.

To be of benefit to the horse, the handler must understand the basic principles of forward movement and be able to lunge correctly with the horse under control. The horse, if not used to lungeing, must be taught to understand the voice and be obedient so that he responds to the handler and goes forwards calmly and confidently with a good rhythm.

He must be taught to carry himself in a good shape by use of side-reins so that he is working and building up strength and muscle. Side-reins will also keep him under control if he is feeling a bit over-exuberant. He must go forwards into a proper contact, just the same as when ridden, and by using the lunge whip to compensate for the legs, you will be able to keep the horse up together.

Watch your horse as he changes from one pace to another to make sure that he is going forwards at all times, whether it is an upward or downward transition. Don't let him fall into a trot from canter, but steady him with the rein and be ready with the lunge whip to drive him forwards into a good, working trot. When wanting to go up into canter again, make sure that he responds as you want him to and listens to your voice and aids. If he doesn't, then practise transitions using your voice until he does pay attention.

Long reining

Some horses are particularly difficult on the flat because they are unhappy or uncomfortable in their mouths. Having first made quite sure that there is no problem with the horse's teeth, which can be the prime cause of trouble, it may well be that long reining and going right back to the beginning would be the answer.

Long reining is a method of lungeing the horse with two reins, but is not easy and is best left to an expert to start with. If you have not done it before, it would be best to ask the advice and assistance of a knowledgeable friend until you become a bit more experienced at this. It can be especially useful for the horse who does not go forwards into a contact as you quietly insist by driving him forwards into the bridle with the two reins. It is not necessary to stay on the circle; the horse could be taken out and about, driven forwards round the yard or farm, into the fields etc. once he is obedient and confident on the circle.

Long reigning can be useful to teach the horse to go forwards into a rein contact and is often used when backing horses or re-schooling them. It should only be done by an experienced person

Trying hard at the Pony Club area competition. The rider is in a good position and is looking ahead well to the next fence. The horse, however, is a little on its forehand

Riding position

The rider's position is of paramount importance as if he loses his balance at any point over a fence, this will inevitably affect the horse. The rider must think of really achieving a deep and secure seat and lower leg to be effective and sure in the saddle.

Practising without stirrups on the lunge can be very beneficial, but it is most important that you relax your hips and thighs so that you sink down into the saddle rather than draw up out of it by tightening. Watch that the lower leg does not become floppy but that the weight is pushed well down into the heel. In this way the lower leg becomes firm and effective and should stay close to the horse's side ready for any necessary action.

For flat work, the upper body should be straight and upright with your head up, looking directly ahead. The shoulders should be back, with the arms resting loosely at the sides and the hands carried just above the withers. If you can be lunged and get your basic flat work right, this will be enormously helpful for the jumping.

Exercises

Special exercises can be practised that will help towards the jumping position. Start by shortening the stirrups up to jumping length and then taking the weight up out of the saddle and cantering in the forward jumping position every day. Once you really feel secure and confident that your leg position is safe and effective, try cantering in the same position, but take your hands away from the neck so that you are no longer relying on the reins or neck for support but are balancing yourself through your seat and legs only. This is a particularly beneficial exercise and once mastered will ensure that you are fairly secure regardless of anything the horse might do unexpectedly.

Another exercise that can be helpful for balance and security is riding on the lunge without stirrups, but instead of sitting to the trot, actually rise to it! This is quite hard work, and again you must be careful not to rise out of the saddle too much – just close the knees and try to rise in rhythm to the horse. Don't overdo this or you will be crippled the next day!

Spiralling in and out of the circle is a useful

exercise as it encourages the horse to supple and loosen in his back and helps the rider to become more effective. The horse needs to increase the bend on spiralling in and to become more engaged with the hind legs, so the rider should do a half halt in preparation before asking for greater flexion. The circle can be decreased to a size suitable for the horse's degree of training and then he should be pushed away into a larger circle with the rider asking for greater collection, whilst pushing the horse into the outside hand as the horse moves away from the inside leg. Practise doing this two or three times on either rein.

This exercise can also be done in canter, when the rider will really need to get the horse back on his hocks to be able to remain in canter as the circle gets smaller. It will really make the rider work to keep the horse's hocks active so that he can carry himself and keep in balance when negotiating this exercise.

Doing any of these exercises without stirrups is helpful to build up your muscles. Keep your horse up in front of you with a strong leg, pushing the horse forwards into a restraining hand.

The flying change

The flying change is a very important exercise requiring a certain amount of balance and impulsion to execute it correctly so that the horse simultaneously changes legs both in front and behind.

There are various different ways of achieving this, but one method commonly used by show jumpers is to place a pole on the ground across the arena and canter the horse up to this on one rein. Then, as you canter and change the bend over the pole on the ground, you make a definite effort to place your weight on the other side, and with a strong leg aid over the pole, you 'shift' the horse onto the opposite leg. Most horses will soon come to understand what is required and will change over the pole as long as you are definite and give a half halt before attempting this. Once the horse changes over the pole, this should then be removed and the rider must make an obvious indication to the horse as to what is expected and where with this help.

The more normal dressage method of teaching a flying change consists of, firstly,

This rider is competing at Wembley in the Dressage and Jumping event. Good marks in the dressage as well as a clear round in the jumping are required for success

ensuring that the horse is collected and balanced by preparing him for the movement with a half halt. To change from the right lead to the left, you must then allow your left leg to move a little forwards whilst your right leg comes back at the moment of suspension and pushes him almost onto the other leg with a slightly lighter and more forward seat. Ride the horse forwards in balance to keep him in this new canter. This is best attempted across the short diagonal, such as turning towards B or E in your arena. Other places could be across the diagonal and change just before you hit the track before the corner. The secret is to prepare your horse in plenty of time and, to start with, to be very definite with your aids. The use of the body can be helpful to teach this to the show jumper if the horse is not terribly well schooled, and you may need to change the bend rather more positively than, perhaps, the dressage world would like to see!

The flying change is vital to success as you move further up the ladder, as it saves time when jumping a round and looks very professional. The horse should anyway be able to perform the simple change of canter to walk and back to canter on the opposite leg. To do this he must be obedient and stay round between the rider's hand and leg on the bit.

Open fronted boots, as seen on this horse, are excellent protection for the tendons. However, don't make the horse immune to feeling the fence should he hit it, because this can lead to carelessness

Control

As show jumping demands precision, it is absolutely essential that the horse is under proper control and obedient to the rider's aids. The correct tack to achieve this becomes vital for success.

The bit

The bit you choose must ensure that the horse has this control but also that he is happy to go forwards in it with your style of riding. Too often horses are abused by their riders who are too strong and rough with their hands for the type of bit being used. It is the hands at the end of the reins that make the bit used mild or severe.

The snaffle in all of its various forms is the bit of choice. There are numerous sorts, such as the rubber, plastic, vulcanite, loose-ringed, eggbutt, straight, and half-mooned, which are all fairly mild. Then there are the French link, Dr Bristol, Fulmer and Scorrier (or Cornish) and rollers of various sorts, which are more severe. Then there are the gags, which come with various different bits to turn them into really strong bits, giving control by their action of raising, yet containing, the horse through pressure on the poll as well as the mouth.

There are also the curb bits, which all have curb chains to increase their action. These include the kimblewick and the pelham in its various forms. The latter can have two reins or one attached to a rounding, as preferred. The curb chains, which should be put on so that the reins give a 45-degree angle to the bit when they are used, come in single or double chain, elasticated, leather or with a rubber cover to enhance or detract from their action.

The double and bitless bridle

The double bridle, which combines the action of the snaffle and curb bits, is an extremely versatile bridle. In the correct hands, it is possible to use each rein independently as long as the rider's leg and seat is utilised to produce the right amount of impulsion to ensure the horse will 'carry' himself. In the wrong hands, or

with someone who does not understand this bridle, it is best avoided.

The bitless bridle is another very useful bridle, which can be particularly successful with the horse who has a very difficult or spoilt mouth. Occasionally, some horses have had such a bad experience with a bit in their mouth that they really become unmanageable, whilst others just simply don't or won't accept a bit, and this can be the answer. There are various types but they must be tried out and checked that they do not rub the horse. The rider must remember that steering will be achieved through neck reining rather than from the direct rein pull, so must adapt his riding to take this into account. It will require a little practice to start with.

The noseband

The type of noseband can influence the action of the bit considerably. For a horse with a light mouth, the cavesson noseband is all that will be required. A drop noseband can make a big difference to the horse who tends to resist and open his mouth a lot. This should be high enough to avoid interfering with the nostrils and breathing of the horse. The flash, a combination of cavesson and drop, is again useful for the strong horse, and the grackle or cross-over noseband helps to prevent the horse from crossing his jaw, which is quite a common problem. To be effective, it must be tight enough to prevent the horse from doing this.

With all the above nosebands, it is necessary to experiment a little to see which one makes the most difference. Some will have quite a dramatic effect whilst others will not make much difference, so perhaps a change of bit combinations is required.

The martingale

Martingales can again be useful in helping with control. The standing martingale will prevent the horse from getting his head up out of the angle of control, but must be correctly adjusted so that it will not interfere with the horse's jump. This is particularly useful for the horse who has a high head carriage, or has been badly schooled and tends to get his head up as a means of escape. The standing martingale may

Allowing the horse to lower and stretch his neck and back muscles is important at the end of a schooling session or at any time after a period of work

only be attached to the cavesson part of the noseband fitted above the bit. It must never be used too tight so that it interferes with the horse's natural jump.

Running martingales are particularly useful in helping with steering, as well as controlling the angle of the head. They should only be tight enough to prevent the head from getting out of the angle of control. Rubber or leather martingale stops must always be used on the reins to prevent the rings from becoming caught up on the billets, which could cause a very nasty jolt and damage the horse's mouth.

Market harborough reins

Market harborough reins may be used, but only in conjunction with a plain snaffle. These reins are designed in such a way that if a horse's head gets too high, the market harborough rein (which is attached to the reins through the bit from the martingale) comes into action to help bring the head down. If the horse's head stays down, it does not affect the horse's way of going. For pony competitions, market harboroughs, bitless bridles and hackamores are not allowed, so it is important that children are found a suitable and effective bit so that they are in control in the ring.

Jumping training

Once your horse is working well on the flat and over poles, you can start to concentrate on jumping. This, however, must not be attempted until the horse is fit enough to take the work. At least six weeks' work is necessary for the horse who has come in from the field totally unfit before he should be allowed to jump.

Using this as a rough guide, you can then decide whether your horse requires more or less slow work and schooling before jumping him. Whatever you do, remember to build up the work gradually and not to overjump your horse at any stage.

Any jumping lesson should start with a small warm-up fence such as a cross pole which encourages the horse to jump in the middle and concentrates his mind before bigger questions are asked

Grid work

Grid work is one of the most useful ways of teaching your horse to look after himself and to develop muscles, balance and general ability. The poles you have already practised over will have settled your horse and he should by now be respecting these and be obedient and alert to the different demands being placed on him.

With all grid work, it is important to build up gradually and not suddenly to ask too much or to confront the horse with a mass of confusing poles. Start off by trotting over the poles on the ground and gradually introduce a fence at a time. A pole followed by a cross rail is the usual start. This can then be followed by another pole and then a small parallel. The cross rail will encourage the horse to pick up well in front and then the parallel will help him to stretch and bascule (round his back) over this wider obstacle. If you have room, another pole or two

on the ground followed by a high cross rail will help the horse to rebalance after the stretch of the parallel. A bounce could be introduced next to really make the horse think and back off a bit, so perhaps a single rail or similar cross to the previous fence could be used. Put a rail on the ground a stride away to finish this and add another parallel, which can be bigger or wider, or a little of both.

The size of the fences depends entirely on the standard of your horse and your own experience. The important thing is to start out with the intention of creating a really confident horse whose ability is utilised by learning to use himself over a variety of different fences.

The distance between the different fences and poles on the ground needs to be carefully worked out to suit your horse's stride. Generally, I find that if you set them 3 m (9–10 ft) apart all the way through, allowing a little more room for a bounce and long-striding

The placing pole used here in canter is a useful aid to encourage the horse to snap up neatly in front. It is no longer allowed for warming up, however, so it can only be used when schooling at home

horses, you will not be far out for the average-sized horse.

The poles on the ground will help to steady the horse in most cases, but occasionally you will come across one who rushes at this build up of fences, almost as if to say, 'Help, let's get this over with as soon as possible!'. Others are rather over-exuberant anyway and just can't wait to have a go. In either case, it is worth spending some time by walking on a circle over the first pole and then trotting over it until the horse has settled down. Do this in both directions and when you decide to go up the grid, try mentally to sit quietly and as calmly as you can so that you do not excite him in any way by the way you react yourself.

Never jump up a grid too often. Twice over each new addition is certainly enough and if the horse has done it correctly and seems confident the first time, there will be no need to do it again – go straight on to the next exercise.

If the horse is finding the grid easy, then raise it, starting with the last fence, and gradually work your way to the first element. Spreads could be widened, but remember that this will reduce the distance to the next fence; the fence will then need to be moved the appropriate distance away. It is most important to remember that with extra height, the horse will need a little more room to be able to negotiate the grid. If he is an experienced horse or one who you want to teach to shorten his stride, then you could leave the grid distance as it is or just ease the last distance a little. As long as the horse is physically able to cope and is learning to use himself properly, then this can only be helpful.

Some horses 'back off' a grid and so need to be ridden forwards more strongly over it so that they do not frighten themselves by having to reach for the fences. It is most important that the horse is encouraged forwards and made to

This horse is not on the bit, so will not be able to work from behind. The rider will need to push him together from her leg into her hand before attempting a jump

lengthen the stride coming into the line of fences. He will otherwise be in trouble when he has to jump a treble on a course.

Jumping single fences

Your horse must be able to jump single fences out of trot and canter, taking just as much trouble to clear these each time. It is important, therefore, to keep his interest and have a variety

of fences to 'pop' over. These should include spreads and uprights, gates, walls, planks or whatever, so that the horse becomes thoroughly accustomed to the different types of fence.

The show jumper should also be asked to jump ditches, logs, hedges, etc. when out on a hack. This will all be good for his education and ensure that there will be nothing that will frighten him or take him by surprise. Even Olympic horses have been caught out by the inclusion of a water ditch in a course, which would not have worried them had they been

The wall requires accurate and controlled jumping, for the slightest tap will usually remove the top slabs. Its solid appearance, however, helps to encourage the horse to respect it

This gate with its curved top is rather kinder than the usual type. All gates should rest only on flat cups and never in the deep ones designed for poles

properly schooled during early training and learnt to accept whatever came their way.

Some horses are worried by patterns or certain colours on the fences; others could not care less. But all horses should be made to jump over unusual objects such as barrels, tyres and straw bales. Other useful ways of getting the horse accustomed to strange sights are to drape your coat or coloured blanked over the fence. Keep the fence fairly small when you do this the first time so that the horse gets over it even if to begin with he does think it is horrifying. He must learn to jump without question everything

you ask him to if he is to be a reliable performer.

Although you should not be required to jump a water jump until you reach a fairly high standard, it is quite possible that one may be included in a class, so the sooner your horse becomes used to this type of fence, the better. If you know of one near you in the area, try to go and jump it, preferably with another horse, just in case you have difficulty. If, however, this is not possible, you can improvise a quite satisfactory water jump from blue plastic fertilizer sacks, laid on the ground under a

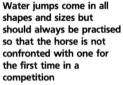
Water jumps come in all shapes and sizes but should always be practised so that the horse is not confronted with one for the first time in a competition

Planks such as these with no ground line and an 'airy' appearance make it difficult for the horse to judge a good take-off spot

fence. If possible, these should be secured in position, either with a pole on top or by some other effective method. You can change the fence around so that the 'water' is before, in the middle or after it.

The ground line

The ground line is important, as it is the point from which the horse judges his take off. The horse assesses this from the base of the fence and if there is a well-defined ground line, this will make it easier for him. It can be pulled out a little when training if the horse tends to get too close to the fence.

False ground lines are confusing to the horse and should not be used. In this case, the ground line is behind the vertical such as if a gate were leaning away from you. This could well encourage the horse to get far too close for take off and then take the whole fence with it. Never take risks – such action could cause a serious accident.

The take-off platform

The take-off platform is the point at which you require the horse to take off to clear the fence easily. Generally this is about the same distance away as the height of the fence, but as the fences become wider and higher, it tends to need to come in closer to the fence. If the rider has a good 'eye' he can help the horse to reach the right spot for this by lengthening or shortening a little on approach.

Jumping a course

The next stage is to make sure that you and your horse are able to jump a complete course of jumps. This sounds easy but in fact requires quite a lot of effective riding so that the horse meets his fences correctly and in good balance to be able to clear them. The approaches and turns into and away from the fences require a lot of pratice to get them right every time if clear rounds are to be achieved.

Try to build yourself courses that flow on but also demand control. A figure of eight is a good way to incorporate a couple of changes of rein.

Include uprights and spreads as well as a double and, if you feel ready for this, a treble at some stage.

If you do not have the facilities to do this yourself, there are usually several shows in the area, especially in Britain, that hold classes of a very low standard if that is what you feel you require, or clear-round jumping classes in which rosettes are handed to those who achieve a clear! You can, of course, if registered, go straight into the affiliated classes, which are generally of a higher standard.

The important thing about riding a course in the arena is to make sure that your horse is able to do what is expected of him; until you have ridden a few courses and obtained a picture of his capabilities, it will not necessarily be totally apparent which areas need working on. Ask yourself the following questions. Is the control right? Do you meet the fences correctly? Does your horse tend to get too close or take off a bit far away? How does he cope with the combinations: is he tending to gain ground or lose it through these, and does he lengthen or shorten his stride? Are you able to keep up a nice, flowing rhythm, or is it a bit jerky? Does the horse keep falling back into a trot?

Any of these problems must be assessed and worked at before you aim for bigger fences, although if your horse is a bit impetuous and this is the reason that one or two of the above are occurring, very often the bigger fences will help to concentrate the mind.

How to jump the course

Assessing how to jump the fences and course is always quite a difficult decision as so much depends on your horse, the course, the ground and the experience of both of you. The most essential thing is to concentrate fully on everything you attempt so that you give the horse every help possible and mistakes are rarely made. In this way, confidence quickly builds up. If the course looks easy, then use it to full advantage to try to perfect the way you turn your corners and make your approaches; keep a continuous rhythm and start to take a few 'risks', which will be necessary to win.

Risks can include 'angling' a fence very slightly, to save time, remembering to start with

This rider is turning his horse whilst in the air, but he maintains perfect balance by keeping even weight in his stirrups

to do this only over verticals. Angling a parallel makes for a big, wide fence and is generally not advisable unless your horse has exceptional 'scope' and can do this with ease. You can also practise speed over some of the fences. Don't forget that the faster the horse goes, the flatter he may jump, so you will really need to keep him together, pushing with the leg all the time into an even, soft but restraining hand so that his jump goes 'up' enough to clear the fence.

Different types of fence

The different types of fence require assessment as to their difficulty, with certain points taken into consideration. These will always include the size and location of the fence, the state of the ground and the presence or lack of a good ground line.

The upright fence should be approached steadily, with plenty of controlled impulsion. If it

51

This narrow fence requires accurate riding and is designed to test obedience. Do not be caught out by not keeping the horse firmly on the track to jump the fence with ease

looks rather airy, you must indicate to your horse that he must concentrate and treat this with just as much care as the more robust fences. It is the flimsy obstacles that get knocked down. Allow the horse to use himself over the fence and don't restrict his jump in the air so that he drops his hind legs onto it at the crucial point. Freedom with the hand over the top of the fence is vital.

Ascending fences, such as triple bars, hog's back (one raised pole between two lower ones), etc. are easier to jump in that they slope away from the horse, and these should be ridden at a sensible pace to enable the horse to clear the height and spread. Don't turn into them too short, but give yourself room to allow the horse to assess the fence; come into it balanced and with impulsion so that the horse does not take off too far away and is able to stretch over the top.

The true parallel is the fence that demands greatest accuracy, as the horse must neatly jump the height as well as the spread to clear it. Always get straight for this, balance your horse and push him into a 'bouncy' stride at the right speed so that he has the impulsion to jump neatly into the air and stretch.

It is vital that the horse can cope with the combination fences and that the rider rides through a combination with the right degree of balance and impulsion to cope with the striding. A double with two strides between the two fences is not too demanding, but when this becomes one stride with a spread to an upright, a little more control will be required. Even more will be necessary if this then becomes a treble with another vertical.

The horse will need to maintain his impulsion and speed throughout the obstacles, and the way he reacts will very much depend on how the rider tackles these fences. Straightness is essential and must be maintained throughout the two or three fences, with the rider encouraging the horse forwards if he is hanging back a bit, or sitting up a little more to balance him if he is tending to go too fast. The rider must ensure that he co-ordinates the movements throughout with that of his horse. He must never pull back with his hands, but must keep the correct amount of balance and impulsion through a stronger leg into the hand.

Doubles, and in particular trebles, are demanding and cannot be practised too often, but large fences need only be jumped

An upright with ditch behind. It is worth practising with poles over before and after ditches so that they will not surprise your horse whenever they appear

A big oxer with ditch underneath. It is important that your horse is used to ditches so that he is not surprised by one in the arena

occasionally, just to keep the horse's (and rider's!) eye in. It goes without saying that the horse must be fit and physically strong enough to jump any big fence or corner of fences.

If you are having difficulty in jumping fences without remaining in the correct position, then a spell of jumping without the reins can be very helpful, as long as you do this in an enclosed space on a horse who is sensible and with someone to help and advise you. Always have a neckstrap or martingale just in case you lose your balance. Either go down a grid of fences with your arms down at your sides or resting on your hips, or have your trainer keep you on the lunge and pop you over a fence a few times in either direction. It will help your seat and control as well as your balance over the fence.

As you progress and become more confident that bigger courses are within your capabilities, remember that there are other classes you can be aiming for such as relay, speed, puissance, etc. You should be able to assess whether your horse is showing any particular aptitude for a certain type of course. Some are excellent for speed, others disastrous, and their qualities can affect the way you ride them in serious competition.

Parts of the jump

If everything has been going well up to now and you are really convinced that you and your horse are sufficiently well motivated to take on serious jumping, then it is also time to study exactly how the horse uses himself over the fence and how the rider's position can influence this for better or worse.

The jump can be divided into four main parts: the approach, the take off, the moment of suspension and the landing. The horse and rider need to be in complete harmony throughout and it is worth studying what the horse does during this period and how the rider should be helping the process.

The approach

The approach is the most important part, as if this is not accurate or balanced and the horse is not concentrating on the fence, the jump is not going to be very successful. The horse must look forwards towards the fence whilst the rider should control him with the hand and push the hocks underneath ready for take off with a strong, active leg and deep heel. Just before the

A good approach with the horse going forwards is essential. The rider is sitting up and driving the horse forwards well out of the turn

A balanced and forward going approach with the rider sitting up in the driving forward position and her leg firmly on

Still going forwards well, even if the horse has got a little long; the rider has maintained the contact well

The take off: the rider has gone forwards well with the horse but has lost the security of her leg by allowing the weight to come out of the heel

A good jump over the fence

Having landed too much on his forehand, the horse will find it difficult to rebalance himself for the next stride. The rider is too far forward and does not have her weight sufficiently down into her heel to drive him up into her hand

take off, the rider will soften his hands so that the horse is free in front and can stretch forwards as the rider's legs push the horse's hind legs towards the take-off point.

The take off

The take off occurs as the horse raises his head, neck and shoulders off the ground and is propelled upwards by the force of the hind legs. During this stage, the rider must sit quietly in the saddle and be sure not to get in front of the movement. As the horse springs upwards, he must go forwards with the movement of the horse, remaining in balance, and allow freedom of the arms to give the horse the rein he requires at this stage.

The moment of suspension

The moment of suspension is the time when the rider must take special care to remain in balance as the horse performs an arc over the fence and prepares to land. The firm leg position with weight down into the heel ensures that the

rider is well supported and able to maintain the correct position. In this position the upper body is able to go forwards so that it is almost parallel with the horse's back and neck as they pass over the top of the fence, and then starts to come up again as the horse prepares to land.

The landing

The landing is the most difficult time for the horse, as he lands with one leg momentarily touching down before the other; during that time he has his whole body weight plus that of the rider to cope with before he takes the next stride. Then the balance is shifted back again, ready for whatever is next to come. The rider can help the horse on landing by sitting light in the saddle and allowing his arms to follow as the horse makes a rather long stride before getting his balance fully under control. The rider who sits too far forward or too far back at this stage is no friend to the horse! In fact, being badly out of position may easily injure or strain the horse by putting too much weight on his ligaments and muscles.

Continuing the basic training

Remember that to succeed at the top, the basic training of the horse must be continued and built on. Keep schooling the horse on the flat, working particularly on keeping the horse's head down and on the bit so that he becomes more and more obedient and finds it easier and easier to lengthen and shorten his strides to the rider's commands. Gradually he will acquire more and more impulsion, which can be released into the explosion of power that is necessary to clear the fences.

Gymnastic exercises

Your gymnastic exercises can be continued, but special emphasis should now be made on how the horse copes with different strides between fences and parallels. Using distances of one, two and three strides will be helpful, especially if you vary the distances slightly so that the horse has to shorten over one stride fence and lengthen a bit to jump the next. Remember, however, that your distances should never be so much that they trap or confuse the horse, but just enough to make the horse think and to encourage him with effective help from his rider to lengthen or shorten a bit as necessary to cope.

Loose schooling

Loose schooling can be a useful way of schooling the young horse, of assessing the horse's technique over a fence, and just of giving a bit of variety to the training programme. For this, you ideally require an enclosed jumping lane, but it is quite possible to make one in a fenced arena by improvising with barrels or jump standards and uprights.

Set your jumps so that they are well spaced out to start with at distances for two, three or four non-jumping strides. Once the horse is used to what is expected of him, you can introduce more difficult sequences and build up grids so that he uses himself well and learns to shorten or lengthen his stride without the rider's help. It is necessary to be ready to drive the horse on with the lunge whip if he starts to hesitate so that he does not frighten himself or

fail to have enough impulsion to jump the fences. Don't overdo the jumping and reward him when he has done well. Don't let him become overexcited or gallop around madly through over-vigorous use of the whip, but just keep calm as you would when doing normal lungeing. If the horse is obedient to the voice, you should be able to control him in this way.

Lungeing

Lungeing over fences has its disadvantages unless done by a professional, as it is very difficult not to pull back on the lunge rein at some stage during the jump. However, the occasional jump over small fences off the cavesson only adds interest to the horse's everyday routine. Put your fence up against the side of the arena with a sloping pole up against the top of the jump so that the rein will not become caught up on the fence as the horse jumps.

Follow along with the horse, being sure that you do not interfere in any way with his jump. It is best to move down a little so that the horse actually approaches the fence on the straight and then really loose the rein as he lands to ensure he does not get a jolt from the rein. You may have to move quite fast and then gradually pull him around. It is quite a good idea to jump him towards the corner of the school so that he will then start to turn himself rather than you having to pull him around.

Jumping at speed

To win classes you will have to learn to jump at speed. This should not be attempted until the horse is jumping well normally and has mastered the technique of jumping clear and easily over all types of fences.

The rhythm and consistent way you ride round a course will determine how fast your round actually is, and very often it is not the speediest-looking round but the quietly ridden tight turns into and away from a fence as well as the ability to angle fences, that will decide the results. How you angle a fence and the speed of approach needs practice at home over smaller fences. Try to keep coming into your fence without checking or pulling at the horse. Just keep your leg on and sit up on the turns, then drive on towards the next fence, keeping a good, consistent feel on the reins. As you walk the course, look to see where there is a short cut to be taken and if you can lose a stride anywhere on your way round. Valuable seconds can be saved if you work at it and think of trying to cut at least a second off every fence by the way you turn or miss out strides. Where you would normally balance the horse with the hand, think more of sitting up and just riding forwards on longer strides. It is amazing how much can be saved with a little determined effort.

Small, nippy horses are usually especially quick if they are allowed to be, whereas the bigger horse does have more problems negotiating turns, though his big stride can compensate for this. Determination and the all-important will to win plays as big a part as any once you have achieved the all-important clear round.

Potential problems

Problems that occur are usually a reflection of the training of the horse, and whether this is due to your efforts or something else needs careful thought. The problem may be a simple one or it could be the start of a serious problem. The important thing is to sort it out there and then, if possible, so that it does not become a major drama but something that can be discounted soon afterwards.

Refusal

The most usual problem that occurs is a refusal, and this can be due to several reasons. Generally, this tends to happen if the horse is being overfaced, particularly if he is a young horse. In other words, the horse is confronted with bigger fences than he feels able to jump at that particular stage of his training. You must ask yourself why he stopped. Was it because the jump was in fact too big? Did you make the approach to the fence too difficult because you

were at an angle? Did you ride with insufficient determination for the horse, whose concentration was wandering a little, to take in sights and sounds? Were you in front of the movement or behind it and so interfering with the horse's natural jump?

Any of these reasons could have led to the horse refusing, but if you have brought on your horse carefully and have built up his confidence, this should not have happened. He should be capable of making the effort and jumping the fence on the second occasion if you really sit up and ride him correctly and strongly at it. The sooner you can solve the problem the better, but at the time remember not to panic or to become discouraged. Give the horse a chance, take him right back so that he can make another approach with plenty of room and then ride him over it. Nothing is worse than a horse who refuses because he is unsure of what to do and has a rider who is equally lacking in confidence. At least one of the partnership must be positive, and the rider is the one who is meant to be in charge of the situation!

Rushing at a fence

The horse who rushes can also be a problem. By dashing at his fences the animal will not be able to jump properly and use himself over them. Try to assess why this is happening. Is it because he is worried, or because you are worried and getting uptight yourself, communicating this to the horse? Or are you frustrating the horse by holding him back too much so that he is worried at not having enough freedom to jump the fence? Any of these or other reasons can be causing this problem. He may even be a bit strong for you and knows that by dashing with his head up he can get away from you, and is making full use of his discovery, knowing that it worries you!

Go back to grids or trotting over single fences. Another idea that often works is to have a raised pole between 30cm (1ft) and 45cm (18in) high, approximately 3m (9–10ft) away from a parallel fence. Jump this off the circle, sometimes just trotting a circle, at other times popping over these two obstacles. Do this on either rein. If the horse still rushes, place another raised pole of about the same height on the landing side, 3m (9–10ft) away. Off the circle, you can jump backwards and forwards over this until the horse starts to settle.

Backing off from a fence

The horses who don't go forwards into their fences are usually the rather lazy type – very often with a magnificent, powerful jump. Because of the effort involved in their style of jumping, they start to back off because very often they find it rather an effort to jump if they have not been ridden forwards strongly enough

to compensate for this. These horses can sometimes start to con their riders and it is not until a problem arises and they land in the middle of a parallel that the rider is aware that in fact they are simply not going forwards. A few good, sharp smacks to get them going forwards may be required and they should be pushed on hard over their fences and not be allowed to jump too high but to use this energy into going *forwards* over their fences. Wear some effective spurs for two or three occasions until the horse is going forwards and jumping well around the courses.

Incorrect training will result in hollowness, with the horse jumping with his head up and a stiff and hollow back which usually results in faults from the hind legs

Hollow back

Jumping with a hollow back is usually the result of the horse jumping too fast or being too tense to use himself properly. This could well be caused by the rider coming back on his mouth or catching him in the teeth over the fence, making him worry and throw up his head over the fence.

Start by trotting over fences with placing poles before and after each fence. Jump low, wide parallels to encourage this horse to stretch and lower his head and be sure that you really give with the hands *forwards* up the neck. When doing grid work, keep the distances on the short side so that the horse has to look down at what he is doing. Work on his flat work as much as possible, especially on the shortening and lengthening of stride.

There are numerous other little problems that can occur and will need to be sorted out, but if you take the time to ask yourself why things go wrong, looking at it from the horse's viewpoint, it generally becomes quite clear. Don't forget to look back far enough, however. Sometimes a horse will do an exercise correctly at one time; then on the next outing he will suddenly remember an unfortunate incident such as overjumping, and on approaching a similar situation, which brings everything back, he will stop dead at the last stride or dash at a fence to try to get it over and done with as quickly as possible!

It is said that the horse and the elephant never forget, and sometimes you are left wondering what on earth it is that so obviously worries your horse, whilst you yourself can recollect nothing that might be the cause. But that's horses, and that is what makes riding all the more fascinating as one struggles endlessly to work out what the thinking is in the brain of our equine friends.

COMPETITION

Once the stage has been reached when you can really think seriously about competing you must look around to see where the nearest shows take place. To compete in affiliated classes you will need to be a member of the British Show Jumping Association in Britain, or the equivalent in your country, as well as to register your horse. This is generally done on an annual basis. Horses in Britain are graded according to the prize money won, with grade C being the lowest grade and A the highest. Ponies fall into two grades: JC or JA.

If you are a member you will receive information on all of the affiliated shows in the country, and there are numerous classes held virtually all the year round. Unaffiliated shows are generally advertised in local papers, tack shops and riding schools. During the winter most shows are held indoors, many in the evening.

Make sure your memberships and registrations are all up to date, that you know where you want to go and that the right classes are being held for your horse's standard and experience. When entering be sure to include your registration numbers if required. Show jumping is so popular that you will find it necessary to enter early to get into the classes, especially at popular venues. Be prepared for big entries with, inevitably, some long waits between classes. It is not unusual to have up to a hundred entries or so in the novice-type or Foxhunter classes.

Pre-planning

To get ready for the show there are various preparations to concentrate on before you set off. Firstly check the transport. Is your trailer or horse-box full of fuel, oil and water, with tyres in good condition and evenly inflated? Is it clean and ready to go, legal with up-to-date tax, and insured for whoever is taking the horse to the show?

Is your horse ready, clean and trimmed? Most horses and ponies do not need to be plaited for show jumping at the lower levels but certainly will need to be at the big shows. However, they should always be trimmed, clean and generally looking good whenever they go anywhere. If not already done, trim up your horse, wash his mane and tail if necessary and clean out stud holes ready for the show.

Check over all of your tack, clean it thoroughly and put it ready to be packed. Remember rugs, cater for all weather eventualities and put out travelling kit for the horse to travel in to the show. Also sort out which type of leg protection you want your horse to use. Most show jumpers use over-reach boots with some form of brushing boots. Open-fronted ones protect the back of the tendon from knocks but leave the front clear, so that should the horse tap a fence, he will be reminded to be more careful next time. Ordinary boots or bandages are preferred by many because they give all-round protection to the horse. Whatever is your preference, make sure that it is clean, well oiled, and supple if it is made of leather or has leather buckles. Any sheepskin or 'fluffy' lining should be well brushed to keep it soft.

Make sure you have a haynet, water and buckets and a feed for the horse if you have a long day ahead. You should also include a grooming kit, skip and shovel plus a box of any special bits and pieces. This might contain a first-aid kit; spares such as numnahs, different bits or nosebands; and flu vaccination certificate if required; the rule book; and any correspondence, such as numbers, sent from the show. Don't forget the schedule and directions on how to get there.

Always allow plenty of time as you never know when something unexpected might happen – such as losing one's way (have a good map), punctures (make sure you have the necessary to cope with this) or traffic jams (take coffee to relieve the monotony!). Organisers of some competitions will send you a draw order the day before – if you miss your turn that is it, and you miss the class. Do not ever be lulled into thinking that just because you are drawn, for example, 45th to go there will be 44 competitors before you. There may well only be ten! Show jumpers are notorious for entering classes and then either not going at all or deciding to go elsewhere.

On arrival

On arrival go straight to the secretary and obtain your number, if this has not been sent. Sometimes there are no numbers and you put down your name or initials on the board, especially if entries are taken on the day. Put down your number on the board or declare your intention to run if this is stipulated. You will need to keep checking when the organisers are accepting numbers for this, as sometimes second and third class numbers are not taken until the first one is nearly over. If everyone else is quick off the mark you may find yourself way down the list.

Assessing the course

If you are in the first class you will need to arrive before this starts if you hope to walk the

Walking the course carefully is vital to success. Be sure to concentrate on how you are going to approach each fence

International jumping stars Greg Best and Jo Fargis discuss the course in West Palm Beach

course. Obviously it is to your advantage to do this and to really get a good idea of when and where you need to come off a turn to achieve the best approach, to walk distances in combinations and to check related distances from one fence to another.

If you have to watch from the ring side, watch how many strides another horse takes and assess how that horse's stride relates to your own. Does it find distances a little short or are they a bit long? Hopefully most horses find them about right. Unfortunately there seems to be a tendency nowadays for course builders to make a distance difficult for the horse, which is disturbing, as horses should never be trapped into difficult situations whereby they are forced to overshorten their stride or have to reach too

far for a fence. It is up to the rider to try to get them to the right spot, but if a distance is too difficult this will only result in a lot of desperate, rough riding and abuse of the horse.

When walking the course make sure you are fully aware of the start and finish points and study how and where you intend to approach each fence. Walk the course as you intend to ride it, and ride it as if you intend to clear every obstacle. On the first round the clear is what you are wanting, so give the horse every chance. It is in some jump offs or, of course, speed classes that clears *and* speed are usually required.

Look at the state of the ground – if it is wet or deep this will make the fences more of an effort for the horse and you will need to compensate by having greater impulsion into your fences and particularly through combinations. On very hard ground the horse may well not want to really let himself go and so will tend to shorten his stride a bit, so you must be ready to push him on. If your horse is affected in this way you should discuss with your farrier whether to put pads on his feet or should simply avoid jumping him in these conditions.

The course plan should be displayed in the collecting ring, including details of the class such as time, speed and jump-off course. Occasionally the plan may also show a dotted line between fences, which is an optional route that may be followed without penalty. A full line indicates a mandatory track.

Assess the overall route: is it flowing, twisty, big or small? Work out how you are going to ride the course to get the best out of your horse. You may need a different braking system such as a different martingale or noseband if a lot of control is required, or even a different bit if you have a problem on very twisty courses. Make sure you put your number down on the board to give yourself time to be ready. If you are late you had better hurry – the class will not wait for you!

The warm-up

Warming up is the most important part of the day, as if you hurry this the horse may not really loosen up sufficiently from being cooped up in the horse-box, perhaps on a long journey. A period of walking will give the horse a chance to settle and relax before you put his muscles into serious action. At least ten minutes of flat work should be undertaken before any thought of jumping is entertained, and then you should always remember that schooling is done at home.

The practice fences are there just for a warm-up – not to be jumped endlessly by selfish competitors whilst others are waiting a turn. There are only two fences provided officially, a spread, and an upright, and these must be jumped in the direction indicated by the flags or coloured standards. The red is on your right and the white is on your left. At official competitions

Warming up in the practice ring. This horse is wearing a special pad on the girth to prevent him bruising himself with his front feet by snapping them up and kicking himself in this area. The horse is also wearing a fly fringe

The practice areas are always busy. It's important that you know your rules so that you do not do anything illegal. For instance, only jump the practice fences in the right direction

the penalty for breaking this rule is elimination or discipline via the steward, but it all boils down in the end to a matter of safety.

After some initial flat work ask your helper to alter the jumps as you need. Some people like to start with a cross, others with a vertical and then go on to a spread. Be careful that all your hard work at home is not jeopardised by taking a risk here in the practice ring, especially with a young or inexperienced horse. It is very easy in the heat of the moment to be tempted to take on something more than you normally would at home. The horse may not be concentrating quite as well as usual with so much going on, and it is in these circumstances that things tend to go wrong. It does not take much to put a youngster off, so always play safe. It is better to go into the ring brimming with confidence than to have a nasty fall over a practice fence and then enter the arena feeling utterly demoralised.

Try to work out a simple routine at home and use this as your warm-up at the show. If your helper knows the form you can do this quickly and quietly without the panic of being rushed into something you never wanted to do. Once you have popped over a couple of fences make sure that the horse 'opens up' a little over a spread off either rein. If you are happy with his performance, keep him warm and walking until your turn. Do not let the horse stand around in the collecting ring or he may start to get difficult about leaving his friends and entering the ring.

Entering the arena

Entering the arena for your round is an important part of your plan for the course. You may have a horse who is quite unworried by the occasion and in that case you will simply walk in, trot a circle and canter in readiness for the start. However, your horse may be nervous and uptight and may refuse to enter the ring. If he is young, keep calm and perhaps ask your helper to lead him into the ring, or even get another horse to go in in front of you and then trot on strongly. It is imperative that having warmed up your horse outside, you do not then stand around but keep walking purposefully and then simply walk into the arena when your turn comes. You do not want to have an argument with your horse at this crucial time, so avoid it at all costs and try to make the whole thing a pleasant experience.

If an old horse tries to be naughty, then a firm hand must be taken, but again avoid standing around, and in fact keep out of the collecting ring altogether until it is nearly your turn, so that he is less reluctant to leave it when the time comes.

Some horses may be best entering at walk or trot; others, especially the lazy sort, will need to come in at a good, sharp canter. Relax your horse with a calming pat, having halted and saluted the judges. This can be done by raising your stick in front of your body and nodding your head in salute. Find out before entering the arena whether or not you are to salute.

The bell

The bell will be rung to start the course and it is most important that you are fully aware of what this sounds like on the day. It may well be a horn, hooter, whistle, bell or whatever, but with so many other noises around on the day you must be sure which is your start 'bell'.

The bell will also be rung:

1 to stop a competitor during the course of his round

2 to give the signal to a competitor to continue his round

3 to eliminate a competitor

4 to disqualify a competitor

5 to retire a competitor

6 to instruct competitors who are walking the course to leave the arena.

Once the bell to start has rung you have 30 seconds in which to start your round. Do not over-run this or you will be eliminated, but take

your time to circle near the start so that you approach on a good stride in balance with the right amount of impulsion and pace for your horse to confidently start his round.

The course

The course will determine your plan of how to ride it, bearing in mind the age, experience and ability of your horse along with ground conditions and whether it is the sort of course that will suit your horse. The first couple of fences are generally quite straightforward and may be aimed towards the collecting ring to get the horse going. Being a herd animal by nature, the horse does not like to leave a group and this is particularly noticeable with a youngster, so you must be prepared for him to hang back towards the collecting ring. Positive riding and giving him something else to think about, such as the course ahead, is what is needed.

Carry your stick in the outside hand so that you can use it if necessary as you pass the entrance to the collecting ring. It is most important that the horse is kept together, and especially if he has been hanging towards the exit he will need to be made to concentrate on the next fence in particular if he is not to hit it through lack of incentive.

Some horses are very 'spooky' in the ring and you will need to sit up and keep your horse up well in front of you so that you are always in a safe position should he catch you out. Try to turn his head away from the problem if it is something on the ring side, but be very firm and use sharper spurs if necessary until he gets over this. Practise more at home with 'spooky' fences.

Related distances

Related distances will undoubtedly have been catered for somewhere in the course. This means that fences are placed at set distances from the next one according to the average horse's stride. These distances are generally divisible by approximately 4m (13ft). Experienced horses can cope with short distances but the inexperienced horse requires

A double of uprights or verticals with one stride in between. Some doubles are marked as A and B on the two elements; others are marked just as the number only of that particular fence. They are jumped as one fence

A treble consisting of three different elements with one or two strides in between each requires accurate riding

more room between his fences, as he will be less collected and therefore less able to cope. Once this distance is more than five or six strides there is little relationship between the fences.

Combinations

Combinations need special care, especially on the approach, as unless you come into them straight the horse will often hang to the outside a bit if he has come off a turn. This means you may well be heading for a run out at the second element. It cannot be stressed too strongly how important it is to present your horse correctly so that the two or three fences are directly ahead of him and that he arrives at the correct take-off platform to be able to negotiate the fences with ease. The pace and impulsion are of course equally important.

If the horse lands short over the first fence because he took off too far away from it or put in an extra stride at the last minute and lost his momentum, the rider will really have to drive him on with the legs and keep his seat light so that he can gain this lost ground. Keep thinking and keep looking straight ahead.

Some horses are too bold and may either come in a little fast or just jump out too far, getting too close to the next element. The rider must keep hold to support the horse but keep the leg on firmly so that the horse can engage his quarters to get himself out of trouble. Keep your weight evenly distributed and do not be one of those riders who leans over to one side over the fence. This is disastrous in a combination, as it forces the horse to shift his weight to that side in order to keep his balance, which may well contribute towards a run out.

Keep the horse in a good rhythm with plenty of impulsion throughout combinations, which should always be treated as one fence – in this way you will keep riding forwards throughout rather than treating each element as a single fence.

The clock starts as the competitor crosses the starting line and finishes as soon as he has jumped all of the obstacles and crossed the finishing line.

Riding the course

Riding the course correctly is essential to success, and the general points have already been mentioned. You now have your horse out in a competitive environment, which may be rather alarming for him, so you must compensate for this by the way you ride him. He is likely to require more help from you, the rider, to control the pace, either by riding more strongly or by steadying him a little more.

Be consistent in all you do, and prepare the horse with little half halts to lighten his forehand if he is pulling too hard on the bit, so that he approaches the fences on a nice, bouncy stride. Keep a consistent feel on the reins when approaching your fences and right up to take-off point. Do not 'drop' him at this last important moment before he actually jumps – it is the cause of so many problems.

So often when confronted with competition, riders tend to fall apart and ride in all sorts of extraordinary styles that are totally different to what they have been doing at home. This is of course very confusing to the poor horse, who not unnaturally also reacts to this with uncharacteristic behaviour. Try to remain calm and consistent throughout your round.

For the young horse in particular there is little point in hurrying him, so your first few classes ought to be treated as schooling rounds only. Do not allow the heat of the moment to get to you, but take a few deep breaths before you start and be sure you do *not* hold your breath during your round. You only have to watch a few competitors at novice level to see how many do in fact forget to breathe properly. The effects of this are not really going to be very helpful to the horse! Remain as cool, calm and consistent as you are at home and you will have few worries. Keep up a consistent pace throughout your course. If the horse is on the wrong leg, try to make him change, but if not, it is better to keep going in balance than to come back to a trot and lose the whole rhythm of the round.

At the end of your course make sure you go through the finish before quietly pulling up your horse on a circle and going out of the arena in walk. Do not gallop straight from the finish to the exit – this will only teach your horse bad

David Broome leaps off a big bank on one of his young horses at the Wales and West Showground

manners. Very often the exit is near the last fence at a different place from the entry point – if so, remember to go out this way, and pat your horse as a reward for his efforts.

When things go wrong

There are naturally occasions when things go wrong, and you will have to be very careful to keep your head in the arena and to re-present your horse at a fence so that he has the best possible chance on a second attempt. It may be that he has knocked down several fences or generally been a big disappointment for one reason or another. Whatever the cause, you will need to sit down and analyse the reasons why this happened and where things went wrong, especially if all had seemed fine at home.

Never take it out on the horse in the ring or on leaving it. The horse has a very short memory when it comes to doing something wrong, although he may never forget the experience of being punished. It is pointless and totally immature to take it out on the horse later – he simply will not associate the punishment with whatever problem happened inside the ring.

Certainly if he has stopped inside the ring, pop him over a lower fence in the collecting ring and be pretty positive about it too, but do it straight away. It is of course usually pointless in these circumstances to enter another class, especially if it is bigger, but if you feel that the horse was just a little overawed and your next class is smaller or easier, then with good, strong riding this could well be an advantage. It is so often *how* the horse is ridden that solves or creates a problem.

70

The jump off

If all has gone well and you have achieved a nice, clear round you will be required to jump off. This may or may not be against the clock, depending on the Table or Rules under which the class is being run.

The jump-off course in affiliated classes should consist of at least six fences, or at least five if the competition is indoors. Although these retain their original numbers, they need not be jumped in the same order as in the preceding round. One new fence (which will have been in sight but blanked off during the first round) may be included in the jump off. Competitors are not allowed to walk the jump-off course, so it certainly pays to walk the original course if you intend to win. If, however, the jump-off course has been substantially altered and fences have been re-sited, competitors may be allowed to walk round. The jump-off course will be written in on the course plan. Plan your route and work out where to save time if necessary.

The draw for the jump off will be read out and you should be ready to immediately warm up your horse if you are one of the early ones to go. It is as well to have led your horse around whilst waiting, just in case it is your number that is read out first.

Depending on the type of jump off, but whether or not it is against the clock, the really important point is to try to get another clear round. It is consistency that really matters at this stage, and if your horse learns to be careful from the start it is a great advantage. Galloping round courses too often will only tend to make him flatten and become careless with his fences.

The horse and rider look small amongst the big fences in the arena for this Grade A class

If the round is not against the clock, do not take any risks but get your approaches straight, arriving at the take-off spot exactly as planned, and give your horse the best possible chance at each fence. Some fences will probably be a little higher and some turns may be a bit sharper than in the first round, but keep the horse together with your leg throughout, and treat each fence with equal determination.

For the round against the clock it is again the clear that is important, and for a young horse you will still be likely to do better if you stick to trying to achieve a steady clear rather than pushing your horse on too much when he might easily knock down a few fences. If you have practised angling fences at home you can save a few seconds now by doing this and seeing how the horse copes in the ring. Cut the corners a bit and push on between the fences, but still maintain the rhythm.

The prizegiving

Prizegiving at the end of the competition is of course what every rider hopes will be a happy conclusion to the day. If you are lucky enough to get into the line-up – and you probably will not know exactly where you are placed until near the end – you should be ready to enter the arena. For the prizegiving you must be correctly dressed and mounted, and it is always appreciated if you can make the effort to thank sponsors as well as the hard-working show secretary and helpers.

Competition rules

Other information that might be helpful includes a few tips on rules, which sometimes are not clearly understood until it is too late and you find yourself eliminated or in trouble of some sort or other!

Registration

Registration is necessary before competing in any affiliated competition and notice of this must be made in writing before the horse competes. The owner and rider must also be members of the relevant association under the correct category before they or their horse compete. All registrations automatically expire on 31 December of each year and on change of ownership, and it is most important that only these horses who are elegible should compete if the owner or rider is not to be fined or cautioned. Horses or ponies under the age of four years are not allowed to compete.

Speed

The speed required varies according to the standard of competition, but generally ponies and very novice competitors run at a speed of 300m per minute. 320m per minute is usual for the first round of most competitions up to Grade A and for any held indoors. The speed must be 350m per minute in the first round of a Grade-A competition held outdoors under Table A, and in an adult open when the prize money is £100 or more.

Time allowance

The time allowed is calculated by the judge, who divides the length of the course by the speed requirement as laid down for that competition under Table A. This time will be stated on the course plan and for any jump offs.

The time limit

The time limit is twice the time allowed for competitions judged under Table A and two minutes for competitions judged under Table C. Failure to complete the course within the time limit incurs elimination.

Stopping for the bell

Stopping with the bell has on occasions caused problems because competitors were unaware of the rules. If, for instance, the competitor has been stopped by the judge or stops voluntarily because of a course obstruction etc., he must not restart his round until the bell is rung to instruct him to do so. The rider will be

Identical courses being jumped by the two riders in this Knockout competition at Olympia

eliminated if he continues before the bell, or if he continues after the bell at a point nearer to the finish than where he pulled up. So, after a fall or other delay you must go back to the spot where the problem occurred before restarting your round. Circling after the bell is considered a disobedience and is penalised as such.

It is always best to keep your horse moving in the above situation so that when the bell is rung to continue the course you are ready for it and can go straight off to continue your round.

Retiring

If for any reason you decide to retire during your round such as feeling that the horse is being overfaced, bad going, safety or whatever, you should signal to the judge by raising your hand or whip and leave the arena in walk. You are allowed, if you have refused, run out or

fallen, to jump up to two fences in the arena before retiring.

Sometimes the judge will introduce a standard if there have been a lot of clear rounds. The judge will then retire competitors who have exceeded the standard set on time or jumping faults.

Withdrawal from a round

A competitor who has declared or who starts in a competition may subsequently withdraw from the next round before starting, provided he informs the judge of his intentions.

Leaving the arena

Leaving the arena at any time before completing the course, retiring or being retired incurs elimination. This situation can occur if your horse is napping or you get out of control. You will also be eliminated if you do not leave the arena *mounted* and at the designated exit. If for instance you get off the horse at the end of your round to pick up your stick or some other dropped item, make sure that you get back on again before going out of the ring. Even if you have fallen at the last fence you must remount before passing the finish and leave the arena mounted.

Losing your hat

Losing your hat can result in elimination. You must retrieve a lost hat before continuing round the course or passing through the finish. You will not be penalised for getting off and retrieving it, except by time. It makes sense therefore to make sure that your hat is securely fastened with a good catch, and if it does tend to come off you had better learn to be quick in getting off and on to retrieve it, otherwise you will incur time penalties!

Outside assistance

Outside assistance, whether intentional or not, may incur elimination if, in the opinion of the judge, it might improve your performance. Make sure your supporters and friends keep quiet and do not gesticulate or wave madly during your round. Even if you lose your way they (or anyone else) must not shout to help you remember – you are out there on your own and it's up to you to get it right, the same as everyone else!

However, the following will not be penalised under BSJA rules:

1 medical or veterinary assistance
2 assistance given in the prevention of danger to others
3 picking up and handing back to a mounted competitor his head gear or spectacles.

The following assistance will not be penalised following a fall:

Geoff Goodwin flings his hat away as he dashes to do the driving phase of the ride and drive class – a very popular competition

Pierre Durand of France with Jappeloup, a combination that tasted great Olympic and World Cup success

The Olympia Christmas Show produces some fun competitions, one of the favourites being the fancy dress class. Phillip Heffer stars in unfamiliar garb!

1 catching a loose horse
2 repairing broken gear
3 re-adjusting saddlery
4 picking up and handing back a whip
5 assisting the rider to remount.

I am afraid there has been the odd occasion when an over-enthusiastic spectator has eliminated a competitor for outside assistance, but generally the judge is able to determine the occasions when a competitor has been 'helped' regardless of circumstances.

Showing the horse a fence

Never show your horse a fence either before starting, during interrupted time when the fence is perhaps being rebuilt, or following a fall – this will incur elimination.

There are of course other rules that could affect you and it is most important that you are aware of what means what in your chosen sport by studying the rule book regularly. Always take it with you so that you can keep up to date and are able to look up the rules for a particular class.

Learning from others

Learning from others is one of the best ways of improving yourself. Watch those in your class and try to foresee when things are going to go wrong. If you can judge this with your fellow competitors you should be able to assess when it might happen to you in certain circumstances. Hopefully you will be able to prevent this as you become more experienced and learn the importance of correct approaches and determined but relaxed riding.

Watch the professionals at every opportunity and see the effective way they have of riding a course. It is particularly interesting to see a real professional on a 'green' horse. He will encourage him and give him every assistance on the approach over the fence and on landing, where he will quickly help him to re-balance himself.

Have a look at how professionals cope with problems. It will certainly not be unique to you to have good and bad days – it happens to everyone. What is important is the way you cope with it. Always aim at trying to be better even if you are lucky enough to be winning a mass of rosettes. It may be fine now, but what will happen at the next level? You must be thinking ahead to your horse's future training so that he is building up muscle and power all the time. A top show jumper should be capable of doing most of the advanced dressage movements without too much difficulty.

He should be sufficiently supple and obedient that flying changes, counter canter and half

John Whitaker and Next Milton demonstrate their unique style which has won them so many prizes throughout the world

passes are all well within his capability, and all the time you should be working on improving your horse just as the professionals are doing. In this way you can be working your way up through the grades with a well-trained horse who, with the right amount of natural ability may well be on his way to joining the 'stars'.

The end of the day

When the day is over at the end of the competition, prepare your horse for travelling again with rugs suitable for the journey. Remember that trailers can become quite chilly, especially in the evening as the sun goes down if it is not really warm. Offer the horse a drink before leaving (he should have been given water regularly throughout the day, except for the hour or so before jumping), especially in hot and humid weather. Give him a haynet, if he has not already had one, for the journey home.

Remember to remove studs; collect all your tack together; put everything away as neatly as possible, and pick up rubbish. Check that you have your whip and spurs and that you did not leave a rug or anything else in the collecting ring before setting off for home. This is terribly easy to do, and the show will not appreciate a call the next day to see if it's still there.

On return, make the horse comfortable and give him a well-deserved feed; check his legs and bandage or poultice, if not already done, if the ground has been exceptionally hard or unforgiving. The jumping horse has to put up with a lot of pounding, and proper care and attention will help the legs to last without problems.

Assess your day and see if your future plans seem feasible or whether as a result of the day's activities you will need to alter them. Think about the course and where improvements could be made, and start to plan your week so that these can be implemented in readiness for greater improvement at your next competition.

FURTHER TRAINING, PROBLEMS, AND TIPS TO THE TOP

Further training will help your horse to become better at both his jumping and flat work and this should be a progressive aim. Not only must your horse be progressing, but you yourself will also need to improve and perfect your technique over the fences and around the courses.

Advanced flat work

More advanced flat work should be a regular part of your horse's training. Improve his dressage with greater emphasis on collection so that his centre of balance gradually moves further back and his hocks become more engaged, enabling him to lighten his forehand and use more power from behind.

There are numerous exercises for doing this, but greater emphasis on canter work will help to improve the horse now. He must be really obedient, well between the hand and leg and remain so without argument during your rounds.

Shoulder-in

The shoulder-in movement should be well established, with the horse well able to maintain this down the full side of the arena. Performing shoulder-in on the circle will also prove beneficial, as this will require even greater engagement. Do not over-bend the neck, but control the shoulders with your outside hand. Keep the outside leg on behind the girth to keep the horse on the circle, with your inside leg on the girth to create a lateral bend in the body. Never overdo this, but make sure at the end of your circle that you let the horse move energetically forwards and stretch down again. After all lateral work the horse must be encouraged forwards.

Half pass

The half pass is the next progression; it is similar to renvers and travers but is usually performed across the diagonal. The horse looks towards the direction in which he is travelling. It is best to start this exercise in walk with a circle of 6–8m (20–26ft). Before completing this, make a half halt and then move the horse across the diagonal back towards the track.

To do this, keep a slight flexion in the horse's body towards the direction in which he is travelling – in this instance to the left. Bring the left hand out slightly away from the neck, almost as if guiding it over to that side. Keep the right rein lightly on the neck to prevent too much flexion. With the left leg maintaining that all-important impulsion, the right leg should be placed rather further back so that this moves the horse sideways. Keep the forehand leading and push him forwards and sideways towards the track.

As the horse progresses you can increase the diameter of the circle until you are going across the whole diagonal of the arena in half pass.

The half pass can also be practised in canter, which again helps to engage the hindquarters; having done a small circle you can, once you have returned to the track, in half pass continue around the arena in counter canter or come back to a trot initially if the horse has yet to learn this movement.

Counter canter

The counter canter is an extremely advanced supplying movement, requiring the horse to canter on a bend with the outside leg leading. It is in effect a canter on the 'wrong' leg, but is performed with the horse in proper balance, maintaining rhythm and impulsion whilst remaining on the bit. The horse's outside flexion is maintained in spite of being on the inside turn.

This can be started initially by performing a loop off the track and back on again, gradually increasing the loop until you are doing a large half circle. Alternatively, you can do a half circle onto the track in canter or canter half pass and then continue on round the short side in counter canter. For this, do not go too far into the corner, as this will make the exercise too difficult. Keep a strong seat aid by distributing the weight so that you are co-ordinating your balance with that of the horse. As long as you can maintain the horse's impulsion, but keep him balanced, you should not find it difficult to learn counter canter.

Problems may arise if the horse cannot maintain this, and he might change or become disunited. Apply stronger leg aids to encourage the horse to bring his hind legs further underneath, especially the outside one, which will have to work a lot harder to maintain this outside canter. It is a tiring exercise, and until the horse is physically fit and strong enough, you should not overdo it. Two or three circles or part circles on either rein will be plenty to start with.

Work on exercises such as canter, halt and then into canter again; the halt can be done across the centre line. Sometimes this can include a halt and rein back. You can, if your horse is schooled, canter in counter canter down to halt and strike off again in counter canter. Make sure your legs are effective and your hands are passive and supple. The horse must obey without resistance.

Further jump training

Further jump training to ensure your horse is fully trained to cope with every type of fence is essential if you are aiming for the top. You should, in your early schooling, have introduced your horse to ditches and water, and practising over a water jump will really only be a formality. If you have not jumped a water fence, start if possible with a small expanse of water 1.5–2m (4–6ft) wide and place a sloping brush on the take-off side. A white pole will help to show the horse where his take-off spot should be. Once the horse has jumped this, you can introduce a pole over the middle to encourage the horse to become airborne instead of jumping too flat. A parallel or triple bar can help the horse who does not bascule enough in the air. When approaching water, maintain the normal canter and apply forward driving aids just the last few strides before the take-off point.

Landing on either leg

Landing on the right or left leg over a fence requires a bit of practice but will save precious seconds when it comes to jump offs and saving time. To encourage a horse to land on, for instance, the right leg in canter, the rider must first shift his weight to the right-hand side and look in that direction. The right hand should be shifted slightly outwards from the horse's neck, encouraging it to bend towards the right. And using strong right-leg aids on the girth with the left one behind the girth, the horse will be guided to the right, although the rider must maintain an even contact on both reins. Never, however, fix the left hand on the neck or you will prevent the horse from bending to the right at all. Always ride your horse straight until at the actual fence from which you wish to make your turn, and then only apply the above aids when you are airborne so that the horse changes his centre of gravity onto the side required.

Common faults

Common faults of the jumping rider are plain for all who sit and watch the warm-up arena to see. What is so important is to be aware of the faults and if you are guilty of some of these, to set about putting them right. Most faults occur because of some form of inadequate riding on the part of the rider, so the sooner you can correct the situation, the better it will be for the two of you.

The rider's faults

Lower-leg position

The lower-leg position is the root of the whole seat. If this is wrong, the rider will inevitably suffer at some stage during a round from loss of balance. This will in turn affect the horse. Keep your heels down with your knees and calves close to the horse, and sit firmly in the saddle. Once the heel comes up or the lower leg slides forwards, the rider tends to slide back in the saddle, re-distributing the balance and rather losing control of the situation.

Length of stirrups

If the stirrups are too long, the rider's legs will not be in an effective position and will swing about in an effort to regain balance. The rider will therefore not have a firm seat and will rely on the hands for support. This may be by 'bridging' the reins on the neck, which is bad as it 'fixes' the horse's head, allowing no freedom. The hands may come up too far out of the angle of control, the horse's head will come up as the reins are used as support and he will 'hollow' over his fences. The rider will usually stick his legs forwards and have all his weight in the saddle, really giving the poor horse a hard time.

To correct this, the rider must shorten his irons and practise pushing his weight down into the stirrups. With the heel and calf close to the horse, he must spend time in the forward

This horse has been jumping to the left over his fences. A slanting pole on that side of the fence has encouraged him to jump straight

position with his hands away from the neck in canter to build up balance and co-ordination. When cantering with the seat out of the saddle, it is important that the rider feels secure and that the leathers are in fact short enough in this position, as it is no good judging this when just sitting in the saddle normally.

The opposite extreme is of course to have leathers that are too short, which forces the lower leg back and tips the rider right forwards. The rider then releases all contact on the rein, disturbing the horse's balance at this vital time. The stirrups must be lengthened and the rider taught to keep a longer lower leg and to sit up a bit more over the fence. Using a jumping lane and going down this without reins will help to teach the rider to stay upright in a better position. This must only be done, however, with a quiet horse. The reins must be knotted on the neck and your trainer should always be present.

Rider's hands

The rider's hands are another problem area and this is a difficult one to improve in some cases. The rider's hands should follow the movement of the horse's head and neck and should form a continuous line from hand to bit. Look ahead over your fences and don't be tempted to round your shoulders and look down. This will tip the weight forwards and leave you unbalanced and ineffective.

Some riders are simply born sympathetic to the horse and understand from the start that the mouth is an extremely sensitive area. Used incorrectly, the bit can make it doubly so; therefore tact and 'feel' are important. Unfortunately, there are an awful lot of riders who simply do not have this 'feel', and although it can be learnt to a certain extent, it will be really difficult for them to become sympathetic

Full of dash and enthusiasm, this young rider has given everything with his hands and the pony looks happy, but the security has gone from the leg which has slipped right back

At this point, the rider has 'dropped' the horse in front of the fence, losing all contact. In time, riding like this will lead to refusals. A soft but supporting hand is required

and caring riders. However, this can often be evened out by their outstanding ability in some other aspect.

Quietness with the hands must always be stressed, and it can be very helpful if the reins are held so that they are carried over the hand in the 'Mexican' style. This can make an enormous difference over the fence and on the flat for riders who find it difficult to 'give' successfully. It will encourage the hand to go further forwards over the fence and the rider will not be able to have quite such a tight hand if he becomes very tense.

Rider's balance

The rider's balance is vital, but if the leg position is correct and the hands move with the horse rather then against him all the time, the rider's balance should be easy to maintain. Any sudden body movement should be avoided and the rider must try to maintain a soft forward seat, with the hip and heel keeping a straight line with another continuous line through from the elbow to the hand to the bit. Balance over the fence is fundamental to good jumping.

Rider's mental state

The methods used when jumping courses will dictate how the horse will actually cope with the fences, so it is most important that the rider remains consistent and mentally calm so that this is relayed to the horse. It is quite useless to get mentally worked up before a course when riding a young horse. In this state the rider will tend to rush his instructions to the horse and will be hurried into making imprudent decisions

This rider has shifted his weight too much to one side, causing his horse to twist in the air. Straightness and good balance must be practised for good results

during his round, such as riding for an unnecessarily long stride, cutting corners and not approaching straight – all the points you have been carefully trying to get right at home.

In this state, the hands will come up, the control will be impaired and the horse will panic and shoot off sideways – the rider will then resort to his spurs, whip, etc. It is easy to see how quickly things can go wrong if you do not keep your head.

The horse's faults

Unless the horse is allowed to use himself properly so that he can really 'bascule' over a fence, he will never reach his true potential. Very often the horse requires extra help to improve his technique over the fence such as encouraging him to 'fold in front', to use the correct take-off spot and to approach calmly without rushing and flattening.

Folding in front

To help the horse to fold in front will require a good deal of time preferably jumping loose so that he can get it right to start with without the rider's weight. The horse should be sent around the jumping lane, which should gradually be built up to include bounce stride uprights, then a stride to a parallel, followed by another one a stride away. Then draw in the distances to make the stride between the parallels a bit shorter, which will increase the bascule. The front rail can be a little higher on these as the horse will be encouraged to look lower to find the back rail. By lowering the head, the horse is able to bring up the forelegs more effectively.

Another useful change to the parallel is to raise the front rail two or three holes on one side and to do the same to the opposite side of the back rail. This will encourage the horse to raise his forearms and bring his feet closer to his elbows, so being neater in front. Any problems will of course be helped by more serious schooling on the flat. To really alter a horse's technique, these methods will have to be practised for two or three months before they will become established. Always protect your horse well with boots and over-reach boots.

The take-off spot

Difficulties with the take-off spot usually result from incorrect schooling somewhere along the line, and sometimes the rider is not sure where he should be taking off anyway! At an upright fence, the horse is generally expected to take off the same distance away from it as the height of the fence. For an oxer, this is the same plus half the width. With wider fences such as triples and hog's back it is usual to aim to take off at a distance from the fence that is approximately the equivalent of the height of the top of the lowest element. The rider must understand the principles of this if he is not to confuse his horse, who will probably know exactly where he wants to take off anyway.

Coming in too close to a fence

The curve over the fence is just as important as where the horse takes off. To be correct, the highest point of the jump should be over the top of the fence. At this stage, the horse's wither should momentarily be the highest point if the back is rounded and the head is stretching forwards and down.

If the horse comes in too close to a fence, he will have to make a very steep take off and will more than likely hit the top of the fence on the way up. He may also do this if he madly rushes the last few strides, spoiling an otherwise controlled approach.

There are various ways of coping with this problem and a lot will depend on how much control you have as you come to the fence. A take-off pole will ensure that the horse stands back more. He will have to look down, which immediately improves the situation, and if the pole is placed at a distance from the fence that is approximately two thirds of its height, the horse will be forced to take off early. There are occasions in the ring when you can angle a fence to give more room on approach.

Standing too far back

The opposite problem is the horse who stands too far back and ends up having to reach for his

Annette Lewis's unusual style does not interfere with Tuten's jump, as she manages to remain in balance and does not interfere with his head

fences. This can become dangerous, especially if wide oxers are involved. With this situation, the horse tends to knock the front part of the fence with his hind legs and will flatten as he stretches out to reach the distance. The curve over the jump will tend to be long and flat and the horse will be in serious trouble in doubles and trebles. He will not be able to rebalance himself in time and will either hit the fence or refuse, losing a lot of confidence.

Some horses can manage to jump single fences like this and get away with it to a certain extent, but to consistently get into such a predicament through a combination will take its toll sooner or later.

The placing pole can be used very effectively in such cases, and this is generally placed approximately 3m (9–10ft) or a little further from the fence if approaching in trot and 4m (13ft) if coming in canter. The aim is to get the horse to take off nearer to the fence so that he is able to jump it more easily and correctly. A high cross pole will encourage him to bascule over the fence, as will a parallel, but the rider must approach the fence with the horse obediently on the bit so that he lands over the pole in the right spot to take off.

If the horse rushes and this method does not entirely solve this problem, it may be more effective to raise the placing pole so that it is approximately 27–30cm (9in–1ft) high; in this way the horse will have to look more carefully and will then have to slow down to be able to negotiate the pole. This is best done on a circle for this type of horse, with the rider approaching from the right or left in a figure of eight or simply on one rein until the horse settles before turning onto the other.

Grid work will, of course, help this problem enormously, and this should be done as often as possible; loose jumping will also make all the difference. If more people were able to jump their horses loose, there would be far fewer problems, as the horse would master his own technique and find life so much easier altogether – the only drawback basically being a rider who interferes with all this.

Geoff Billington demonstrates his impression of Annette Lewis's style, perhaps showing rather more daylight between horse and rider than Annette!

Loss of confidence

Loss of confidence is one of the main reasons for various problems that arise but to be able to solve this, you really need to find *the root cause* and the sooner the better, as once a horse has learnt to refuse, it will be very hard to eradicate the habit.

It may be that the rider is lacking in confidence, especially if the horse is young or inexperienced, and we have already discussed this. It is very probable that this same poor horse is being overfaced and is expected to cope with fences or combinations that are above his present capabilities. It takes at least three years of systematic training to bring a horse through from a real novice to a top-flight jumper – and that is in the hands of a professional who knows what he is doing. So you will need to allow even more time unless you are receiving regular help.

There may be something physically wrong with the horse – such as a virus, bad back or pulled muscle – which is hurting him, so you will need to call out your vet to give him a good checkover or the 'backman' to look at his back. The jumping horse has to reach and stretch, twist and turn as well as to jump fences of all shapes and sizes, and it is hardly surprising that this catches up with him at times. It is so important for this reason not to overburden the young horse, who simply will not be strong enough physically to cope with too much.

The ground conditions can easily upset a horse. If the ground is wet and slippery, this can be quite unnerving and you should be sure that your horse never jumps in those conditions without big studs all around. He should also be well protected with boots and bandages as he will be more prone to knocks and bruises on poor ground than on a good surface. Question whether your horse is capable of jumping the course in such conditions. The deeper he goes into the ground, the higher the fences are going to be for him – it only needs one or two nasty experiences for the young horse to be put off altogether.

At the opposite end there is the very hard ground, which will cause jarring to the legs and even the whole body. No horse will want to jump if it is very uncomfortable, so the horse will tend to shorten his stride and not really go forwards to his fences, resulting in some awkward moments. Avoid jumping more than just occasionally in these conditions if you want to keep your horse confident and sound. Do not jump the horse straight away after shoeing, especially on the hard, as his feet may feel a little tender and this certainly will not encourage him to jump. Always arrange for your farrier to come a few days before a competition so that the shoes settle.

The rider who gets in front of the movement and too far forward so that all the weight is on the forehand is a well-known reason for refusals, and if the horse is too inexperienced to cope with this fault on the part of the rider, he will sooner or later start to stop. This in itself may not worry some horses too much, but if the rider also drops the contact, the horse suddenly loses his means of balance just at the most crucial point – his final approach stride or on take off.

Some horses encourage the rider to release too soon because they slow down into their fences, therefore putting too much weight on their forehand, and the rider feels more rein would encourage them to go forwards. This is generally not the case, as these horses are often rather idle and need positive, strong legs to push them up to the bit and forwards. Spurs and a schooling whip may help to solve this sort of problem.

Riders can often be seen over-checking their horses, sometimes to such a degree as to make it impossible for the horse to jump. By doing this, the rider is totally taking over the situation and should he get it wrong on occasions, the horse will have to make sudden adjustments and, after being so restricted, may well lack sufficient pace to cope. Try not to interfere so much in this way and learn to ride your courses in an even, flowing pace, allowing the fences to come to you rather than using too much pulling and kicking.

'Ducking out' at the last moment at a fence can be very unnerving. This is usually caused by lack of confidence at the last moment, possibly because of the rider's position; insecurity; simply being too much on the forehand to cope with the jump; or stiffness. This latter point becomes more and more important as time

The horse is on his forehand and is not going forwards enough, despite the rider's last minute efforts to sit up and release the contact

The result of a bad approach! The horse has too much to do to get off his forehand to jump the fence and decides it's better to come to a halt

goes on. The jumping horse needs to be very supple to be able to jump well and athletically, so any stiffness or onesidedness will eventually affect your horse.

Flat work cannot be stressed strongly enough; both reins must be exercised and the horse must be made to use himself correctly on either rein. He must be made to bend the stiff back and that side just as well as the other. If he is very onesided in his mouth, check his teeth to see that there are no wolf teeth or other problems in the mouth, and then really insist that he starts to work evenly. Remember that if this is a new problem, then there has to be a reason why it should suddenly have worsened, so it is worth checking his back in case he has pulled a muscle or there is something else wrong with the back. Very often stiffness is caused through lack of engagement and positive riding on the part of the rider, who has not been pushing the horse up to the bit, causing him to become a rather rigid, stiff ride. This will not then make it easy for him to jump.

Any of the above will contribute towards a lack of confidence. There are also numerous other reasons, but if the horse has some natural ability and is well schooled, there should be no reason why they should not be overcome. If you have had a problem, it is always best first to step back a bit to re-establish form and rebuild confidence. Sometimes a complete break may be the answer. Turn the horse out for a month or so and let any unseen aches and pains sort themselves out rather than cause too much of an issue over a problem. Nine times out of ten the horse will come back refreshed and rested and ready to start again, with previous problems forgotten, as long as you have not worried him unduly beforehand.

Improving speed

Improving your jumping speed becomes even more important once you feel your horse has reached the point of really going out to win after his steady build up. You will have done quite a lot of jumping at speed at home and during the jump offs for various classes, but it is now essential that you and the horse are really adept at jumping fences on the angle at a faster speed.

You can practise this at home over a figure of eight line. The easiest way to teach the horse is to set up a short grid of some poles on the ground to a cross pole or even a bounce, or cross poles on the angle to one non-jumping stride to an oxer. This needs to be set up so that you can approach it from either the left or right. A second grid to the oxer will therefore need to be set up, heading towards the spread. Start over the poles in trot and then pop the bounce with a canter stride to the oxer. Continue doing this a couple of times off either rein and then remove the poles. Continue to do the remaining exercise in canter over the bounce to the oxer. Remove the first pole of the bounce and then the second. You can now jump just the oxer on a figure of eight.

If you can jump this off a good stride each time, you will find it quite easy to build up a bit of speed, but it is important that your horse is kept athletic and sharp enough to maintain this to the end of the course. He will need quite a lot of weekly cantering when he is expected to do this so that he is physically fit enough in wind and limb to be able to cope. Time and again you tend to see horses start off well around a course but tire towards the end and knock a fence or two. It may only be a short period that the horse is in the ring, but it requires maximum effort and, especially when jumping at speed, the horse will need to be very fit to maintain his neat style of jumping around the course.

The saying that a 'fit horse is a happy horse' is true. There is nothing better than feeling suitably well and able to do the job required. If your horse also looks good, has a bright eye and a glossy coat, is well muscled and neither too fat nor too thin, he should be ready to go, as long as he is also a confident and happy horse. With all this, your horse should be a force to be reckoned with, bearing in mind that you have given him time to mature and to learn how to cope with all of the different types of fence, course and situation.

Straightness is essential for a safe ride down Hickstead's big bank. Eddie Macken is using all his expertise to cope with a somewhat dangerous descent

Aiming for the top

Aiming for the top is the final phase – once you have decided that you and your horse are cut out for this. There are numerous different training courses available around the country but it is important to go to a trainer who you understand and whose methods you can associate with. If you have already had a lot of help from a certain trainer and all is going well, then fine, carry on. But if not, try to improve yourself with fresh ideas from different people, always being careful not to become muddled or confused by too much technical jargon. The important thing is to understand how your

horse jumps and why he can and can't jump in certain styles.

Always remember that short cuts rarely pay in the end, so be very careful if quick methods are recommended. They might well help to win a few rosettes in the short term, but might ruin your horse's style in the long term. Quick success is unimportant; it is the consistent, long-term, gradual build up that will help you and your horse in the end. Having said this, remember that 'if you don't try, you don't get', so it's no good sitting back for too long, thinking it will all come right in the end, because it just simply may never happen unless you set yourself achievable targets each year. You may need to have two or three in case of

Jo Fargis and Mill Pearl demonstrate the tremendous scope required to jump big fences as they soar majestically over this big spread fence

To jump fences such as this, horse and rider will have undergone years of extensive training

problems along the way, but something to aim for will keep you in touch with what you have already accomplished.

Remember that whilst one horse may come right relatively quickly, another may be a real problem and take ages – but if it is any comfort, as long as there is enough natural ability, the difficult ones often turn out to be the very best!

Above all, be a good competitor: take the rough with the smooth, obey the rules and create a good image for show jumping – and enjoy yourself! There are few sports in which so much enjoyment can be had in such a competitive atmosphere. If you can bring on your own horse and learn as you go along, the rewards are great. Therefore, there is no better way of spending your time with a horse than show jumping!

GLOSSARY

angling – approaching a fence on an angle in an effort to save time.

bascule – the rounding of a horse's back over a fence.

bounce – two fences with a non-jumping stride in between.

brushing boot – protective pad to prevent the horse from striking cannon bone or fetlock of the opposite leg with inner side of the hoof or shoe.

cavesson – a strong leather headcollar with rings for the lunge rein, used for lungeing.

cavesson noseband – part of the bridle worn under the cheeks and above the bit.

clench – the point of a horseshoe nail that may often protrude if not kept regularly shod.

curb – the thickening of the tendon or ligament at the back of the hock, caused by strain.

curb bit – a bit with a curb chain usually used in conjunction with the snaffle to make up a double bridle.

curb chain – a chain fitting across the chin groove and attached to the hooks on a curb bit.

drop noseband – type of noseband that fits round the muzzle just below the bit to prevent the horse opening its mouth.

flash noseband – a combination of a drop and cavesson noseband.

flexion – the supple curvature of a horse's physique.

folding in front – the action of a horse picking up his feet and forearms neatly over a fence.

gag – a bit that applies pressure to the horse's poll and pulls up in the mouth when the rein is pulled. It is quite severe.

gamgee – protective padding used under bandages.

grackle – type of noseband that crosses on the front and fits above and below the bit.

hackamore – a bitless bridle, with a single rein.

half pass – a lateral movement where the horse travels forwards and sideways diagonally.

headcollar – unbitted leather bridle for leading a horse or tying up in a stall.

heel bug – greasy or infected heels.

hock – the joint on the hindlegs between the second thigh and the cannon bone.

hock boot – a shaped leather pad with straps, fitting over the hock to provide protection.

hog's back – type of fence characterised by one raised pole between two lower ones.

horsehage – vacuum packed hay.

impulsion – forward movement created by the muscular strength of the hind quarters generated by the rider's skilful use of hands and legs.

kimblewick – type of pelham curb bit used on its own with a single rein.

lungeing – the circling of a horse on a single rein round the schooling area.

martingale – piece of harness attached from the girth to the noseband or reins controlling the movement of the horse's head via the reins or bridle.

numnah – a material or sheepskin pad cut into the shape of a saddle, but slightly larger, to be worn underneath the saddle to prevent pressure in cases of a sensitive back.

overfacing – challenging a horse to jump bigger and/or more difficult fences than he has confronted in training or is ready to attempt.

oxer – type of parallel fence.

pelham – type of curb bit used with one or two reins.

pirouette – movement whereby a horse turns on the haunches in canter or walk.

poll guard – protective pad used to protect the top of a horse's head, between the ears, especially when travelling.

renvers – a suppling exercise with the haunches out.

roller – a girth with two pads for either side of the spine, to keep a day or night rug in place.

self-carriage – balanced movement achieved through the horse's efforts.

snaffle – the simplest type of bit formed of a jointed, or unjointed mouthpiece.

spiralling – suppling exercise whereby the horse moves in circles of increasing or decreasing circumference.

surcingle – a webbing strap passing over the saddle, or rug, to keep it in position on the horse's back.

thoroughpin – a distension of the tendon sheath above and either side of the point of the hock, caused by strain.

travers – a suppling exercise where the haunches are bent round the rider's leg to the inside.

windgalls – soft, painless swellings around the fetlock, caused by strain or overwork.

INDEX